When Godly Women Are Overweight

7 Foundations for Change
and
22 Myths We "Feed" Ourselves

By Christie Miller
Fresh Look Thinking Ministries

When Godly Women are Overweight
7 Foundations for Change
and
22 Myths We "Feed" Ourselves

Copyright @ 2017 Christie Miller

Contact the author through:
www.FreshLookThinking.com
info@freshlookpublishing.com

Book 1:
When Godly Women are Overweight
7 Foundations and 22 Myths
Published, Winter, 2017
Book 2
50 Ways Out For Godly Women
Who are Overweight
Published, Spring, 2017

Scriptures taken from New American Standard Bible (NASB), New International Version (NIV) translation and The Message, and JB Phillips paraphrases.

✳✳✳✳✳✳✳✳✳✳✳✳✳

Dedicated to:

*Joyce Feil,
my dear, sweet friend
and all of the precious
members of my Small Group.*

*They SEE into me and
actually LIKE the VIEW!*

✳✳✳✳✳✳✳✳✳✳✳✳✳

Special thanks go to Kelsey Barnwell of
Kelsey Michelle Photography.com
*for the cover design; to Maddie Meloy and
Jill Sines for editing, to Abby Rockwood Classic
Cupcake Designs, and to Laura Albert
for the spoon designs.*

PREFACE

We live in an amazing time. We have finally figured out what works. Not the 300 new diets out there waiting for you to try, but we have finally figured out what works and what doesn't work for those struggling with weight issues. Seriously!

Research on recovery from food addictions (and many other addictions) as well as new discoveries on the brain combined with the power of God's word have revealed to us:

Why we do what
we don't want to do!
(From Romans 7:15)

That statement is penned by the Apostle Paul in the book of Romans (7:15). Even though this godly man had a close walk with the Lord, he still admitted that he often found himself doing things that he didn't really want to do.

Sound familiar? I have often felt like this! I wake up in the morning, fully intending to eat healthy, and before noon I have gotten way off course. I consider myself someone who loves the Lord, has a strong faith, an effective ministry, and yet, I find myself, "doing what I never intended to do."

WHAT we eat? Some of us just eat the wrong things. WHEN we eat? Some of us just eat all of the time or have occasional out-of-control binges! HOW we eat? Some of us eat fast and have huge portions. WHERE we eat? Some of us love eating out, and unfortunately, fast food restaurants often draw us in. All in all, this "Standard American Diet" that lures us in many ways becomes our downfall.

My desire is to walk closely with the Lord, but in the area of food I let myself and Him down so often. My heart wants to say no to the things that I know are not good for me and might grieve my Lord, but my flesh wins out time and time again. In other areas of my life I see great growth and victory, but this area of weight is a "weighty one" for me.

Paul declares that Christ will set us free, but HOW?

Paul continues on after that admission in Romans to ask, *"Who will set me free? Thanks be to God through Jesus Christ our Lord!" (Romans 7:16)* I have read that statement over and over again. I know that behind every victory is our Lord, but I am very quick to ask "HOW?" when I read this verse.   Paul's answer doesn't really tell us HOW.

Take it from one who has struggled for years (close to 60) with this battle against the bulge, the answer to this dilemma is not quite clear in this passage even though Paul says it with great emphasis.

I know that Jesus Christ is the only answer to sin. He died for our sins, but in the moment of great temptation, what does this verse tell me?   It tells me there is a way out -- a way to be free.   It tells me to be thankful that Jesus Christ has accomplished the way out, but what it looks like to me on a daily basis of flesh verses spirit – good intentions versus the realities of my choices – I'm not quite sure what that means.

There is good news!

The good news is that God has chosen *this* time as a time to reveal to us some new studies on the heart and brain that give us powerful insights into our frustrating defeats in this battle called food addiction.

Honesty,
Nothing But Honesty

In this book, I hope to honestly (with no personal secrets withheld) share with you my struggles and my findings that have been changing my heart – dramatically. I'm delighted that you have chosen to take this journey of discovery with me. Thanks be to our Lord Jesus Christ for His never leaving us "undone."

We'll start with some of the foundational understandings that we need to embrace. Then we will tackle the myths that we "feed" ourselves.

I hope that you feel as you read these pages and take this healing journey that I am right there with you. May God bless you on this journey as He has blessed me.

Christie L. Miller

About the author:

Christie L. Miller is an author, Christian leader, teacher, and heads up Northwest Christian Speakers Bureau as well as a being a speaker throughout the United States through her ministry Fresh Look Thinking. She lives in Bellingham, WA with her husband where she loves to snow shoe, tries to grow a garden on their five acres, and spends time their two grown daughters and her son-in-laws. She also loves her work with Creative Youth Theater, a summer drama program, as well as teaching English classes to homeschooled students.

Contents:

Fresh Look Publishing   Copyright, 2017

MY PERSONAL HISTORY

Our eating problems began at some time in our history. Mine began about age 10 and have continued until 67. As a child I felt lonely, controlled, and as if I could never be good enough.

These three feelings (which I became aware of much later in life) were motivators to my eating patterns. They have produced a definite thread running through my history of unhealthy eating.

I was a food sneaker, and it wasn't long before food became my friend in troubling times. This continued through the stresses of middle school, high school, college, in a challenging marriage, and into my professional life. I seemed to get a handle on it at various times, but then those extra pounds kept coming back – especially after having children.

In addition to this, as I got older, I began to feel discouraged that life had not turned out the way I had hoped or expected. Struggles in my marriage (as much my fault as my husband's), with jobs, and other relationships also sent me back to the kitchen. Soon, I would realize that I had a food addiction, and that in all honesty, I would define myself as a binge eater.

The patterns of running to food when life got uncomfortable were burrowing themselves deeper and deeper into my habits and soul. My choices were often controlled by my difficult and wounding experiences, not by my knowledge, faith, or maturity as a godly woman.

Eating to me is the "sin which so easily besets" (Hebrews 12:1) which J.B. Phillips translation calls the "sin which dogs our feet."

However, God made it clear that this was the year that I needed to finally get a handle on my eating issues through truth and grace, and also that this was the time I should write this book as I logged my journey.

It was over six years ago that the Lord gave me this title and called me to write this book for the Body of Christ. I kept making excuses since I hadn't conquered my issues. Even now, I continue on in this journey, so I don't have a before and after photo for you – YET! I am still a person in process like we all are!

This project has been exciting, encouraging, and full of struggles. Being honest with you in this book has been easy and frightening at the same time since I am a woman in ministry. Secrets aren't easy to tell. I've struggled with shame, guilt, remorse, rebellion, stubbornness, disappointment in myself, and hopelessness.

I've also been met by the Lord with His wisdom and guidance and each new day "full of mercy." My prayer is that my journey and my complete honesty in this book will serve your heart to love and know the Lord more closely as you walk through the realities of your eating issues.

I also pray that your eating issues will be a tool to learn to live more closely to the Lord, just as this "problem" has been to me. As Christian Psychologist Henry Cloud recently said,

*"**Wise people have problems.**
Foolish people have patterns."*

My eating issues have been a pattern, and now I want to face them head on as a problem for God to partner with me to solve. I no longer want to be a fool with patterns that lead to destruction. I am embracing the freedoms the Lord has won for me to face this problem.

Christie Miller

Section One

Seven

Foundations

For Change

In the battle for weight loss and to get healthy, there are seven foundations we need to understand before we can succeed.

Foundation For Change # 1
Discovering The Limbic System

Have you ever felt that an alien has invaded your body? An alien who has a never-ending appetite. You do what you don't want to do, almost like you are in the audience watching yourself do these things. That is exactly how I used to describe my frustrating failures with food.

After decades of struggling with my weight and uncontrolled bingeing, I feel blessed to finally discover that there could be some truth to this idea of "unknown forces" invading my attempts at weight loss success. Maybe not aliens, but when drives to eat, eat, and eat some more hit me, I *have* been *snatched*, so to speak!

I'd love to share with you the turning point truths I have recently discovered on this journey.

*I've asked for so long, HOW – HOW – HOW
can I lose this weight and feel
some semblance of self-control?*

To me, what I am about to share is like the missing link we have all been seeking – the answer to the mystery of why we can't get a handle on our eating issues. Exciting information has surfaced in the last ten years about.....

Why we do what we don't want to do?

In recent years, new and exciting findings about our brains have been presented to the Christian and recovery communities. In fact, this is such an exciting time to be alive because of the abundance of new information that has been discovered about the brain in relationship to addictions and uncontrolled behaviors. Neuro-scientists studying the brain have found there actually is an unconscious part of our brains that drives our behaviors, and sometimes it even overpowers the conscious rational part of our brains. This part of the brain is referred to as the experiential part of our brain, not the rational part.

After spending many years trying to find answers to the weight gain and loss roller coaster and coming up empty (actually not empty but full of guilt and more pounds than I ever wanted!), science is now offering a reason why dieters can't stay on a diet!

Paul asked the above question in Romans 7:15, *"Why do I do the very things I don't want to do?"*

Praise God! We now have some answers to that question.

Michael Dye, author of the *book The Genesis Process*, worked for years with alcoholics with hardly any success. He shares how he was so frustrated with the number of his clients who relapsed that he began to ask God for some answers to this question.   Why is it we say we are *not* going to repeat a behavior, and the next minute we do it again?

Putting recovery principles together with Biblical principles and adding what neuro-science has recently revealed about the brain, Dye's work with alcoholics (and others with addictions like food addictions), we are reaping some amazing understandings. These same truths speak right into our battles with weight. They explain why we do what we don't want to do....eat more than we know we should and eat things we know we shouldn't eat.

The first place we are going to go on this journey is straight to the heart –yes, I mean our hearts. Newest research on the brain has sifted through what the Bible has to say about the heart and has come up with something we never considered before.

Most Biblical researchers of the brain are now considering the heart to refer to a part of our brain as the home of our mind, will, and emotions.

Up until this time the heart has been this mysterious part of our being. It had no real location in our body, so we really didn't know how to scientifically handle "broken hearts" or things like "motivations of the heart."

We ask God to change our hearts, but really don't know what that means "internal organ-wise." When I was in college, I took a human anatomy course, complete with cadavers. As we dissected them, holding the heart, brain, liver, etc., I asked how anyone could not believe in God after seeing the workings of the human body. Then I asked God how His changing our hearts works.

Looking at what scripture tells us about the heart, and examining what we now know of the brain, there is an undeniable commonality.

When we read "heart" in scripture, it is actually referring to a part of our brain. That's all fine and good, but what does that have to do with my binge eating? Plenty! The brain is divided up into many sections, each having its own function or purpose. One part of our brain is our rational side. It is our thinking, logical, knowledge-filled, rational section of the brain. It is where we make our intelligent decisions.

However, there is another part of the brain that will be our main focus for this journey into the weight mystery. My goal is not to get too technical here but to stay practical here. (That's the only way I can understand it myself.)

The front of the brain is the rational part of the brain, but the center of the brain is where we will be focusing. We can call it the "limbic system." (It has various other names, but for our purposes let's stay with this title.)

This area of our brain is in charge of everything we EXPERIENCE in life and our responses to those experiences — from the time we are in utero, throughout childhood, and on into adulthood.

This limbic part of our brain records our experiences as pain or pleasure, hurt or happiness. If you experience pain and hurt, this unconscious part of your brain will go into a "drive to survive" which will try a variety of ideas to protect you so that this pain or hurt will never happen to you again. It initiates a survival system of protection for us.

It will "teach you" or "motivate you," or "drive you" to avoid, isolate, strike back, or take drastic measures to ensure that it doesn't happen again.   If something is pleasurable, the limbic part of your brain will work so you repeat this experience again.

Sometimes, however, we are reacting to pain by putting into our lives a "pleasurable" experience which we have created to avoid the pain –such as binge eating or hitting the kitchen for sweets or carbs – that keep us from feeling pain.   The limbic system is quick to motivate us to do just that!

> *The limbic brain remembers these*
> *pleasurable experiences*
> *(such as bingeing on ice cream)*
> *and will motivate us to repeat that*
> *pleasurable behavior again and again.*

In this way, these pleasurable experiences can turn destructive and defeating to us. Eating for example, can become more than just to fuel our bodies. The limbic portion of your brain sees great tasting food as being a very pleasurable experience that bears repeating especially if it helps you survive something that might be painful. If it helps you numb feelings of hurt or fear, your limbic system will take you there as part of helping you survive difficult situations.   In this way, food helps you eliminate stress.
The limbic system has our survival and protection as its sole motivating force.

> *When hurt or stress comes,*
> *eating comes to mind unconsciously*
> *to put a pleasure band-aid on the hurt.*

This has become such a common response in my life so much so that I don't even know I am reacting to anything. I just move into the kitchen led by some unknown force, you could say. Before you know it, I've devoured a dozen cookies. Then my rational self (which has been overpowered) wakes up and asks, *"What have I just done? I didn't want to do that!"*

Remember that our limbic system operates as the unconscious part of our brain/heart. Sometimes the drives coming from this area of our brain are so powerful, they outweigh the conscious, rational part of our brains. This is why the 12-Step program starts with, *"I realize I am powerless."*

Here's an example. Let's say my husband says something that hurts me, not intentionally, but it hurts. Because of our past marriage difficulties, my limbic system goes into high alert. (It has no idea of time! A hurt yesterday is as powerful as a hurt 35 years ago!)

It loudly says to me "Avoid! Avoid! Avoid! Quickly move to pleasure! You don't want to feel this pain! Quick, get some food to numb yourself." Remember, my limbic system is designed to protect me from pain and hurt. It remembers that eating brings me pleasure, an escape from the hurt as a numbing sensation. That's why food has now become my new "go-to" for avoiding pain. All of this can be quite unconscious. Experience has taught me that going to food is more pleasurable than confrontation.

Hurt also leads me to isolate, so I won't be hurt again. That is like living in denial!

Researchers have also discovered that the limbic system does not respond to words – only to stored experiences. It is just a reactor to provide you with protection from hurt or as a motivator to have you repeat a pleasure. Whatever becomes pleasurable to you becomes your "go-to" behavior driven by this part of our brain. You can tell it not to do this, but it doesn't respond to words, only to experiences.

This is why we can hear so many talks on "eating right" and "changing our habits" and the *words* just don't resonate with our unconscious limbic system. It only responds to experiences, not words. We can also hear about the benefits of confronting our hurtful relationships to repair them instead of isolating from them, but our limbic brain tries to keep us from even taking that type of risk. It could lead to more hurt. Numbing with food is a much more pleasurable way out.

While some people choose drugs, alcohol, spending, judgments, control, perfectionism, work-aholism, people-pleasing (and the list can go on and on), I have chosen food as my new friend. Why not? It is readily available (in most of our lives), and it gives me a pleasure that my limbic system says to repeat and repeat again and again for my survival. The limbic system drives us into this pleasure as a way of life. Soon a habit is formed.

What does this all mean?

When I learned about this research, it made so much sense to me. The years of vows to eat right, starting new diets, pledging that "this is the year," were being sabotaged by my limbic system which was full of unhealed wounds and hurts. I do what I don't want to do driven by my limbic system that is trying to protect me.

I have struggled with this for close to 60 years, and I now see how gradually over the years food became my "go to" to avoid pain and to increase my pleasure -- all very unconsciously. For years, when people told me that I was eating as a comfort, I just didn't get it – until now.

I can make all of the commitments I want to make telling myself that "today is the day" – "eat right" – "lose the weight"– and my limbic system actually fights against me in this. Remember, it doesn't respond to words, only to experiences.

Before this sounds hopeless, realize that Jesus Christ is the way out. He has a way for us to get victory over this. He understands the limbic system. After all, He created it.

This all means that I needed to look further than just at my behavior for change to occur. I needed to look into my heart. It is my heart/brain that is working against me. It took great courage for me to be willing to say, "Okay, if that is what is behind all of this, then I'm going in" – into my heart/brain to see what's motivating all of this.

I have got to find out what experiences are driving me to the kitchen instead of facing my realities. Romans 8:20 tells us that "*sin has made its home in us.*" I see this as sin by us and sin others have done to us that have left wounds. All of these have made their home in our limbic system.

I needed to identify these hidden "sins" before I could begin to work with the Lord to turn it all around. You could call this "getting to the bottom of the problem" – to the root.

I knew this journey would take great courage and compassion from the Lord – that He would be the source of all healing and power to make a change. As I took this journey, I found memories coming to the surface that were painful. From the rejection I felt when I was 10 when Danielle and Pamela told me that they didn't want me to walk to school with them anymore – to the time my first boyfriend broke my heart – to my boyfriend dying in a motor cycle accident – to the disappointments in my marriage. These are just a few of the painful experiences imbedded in my heart/brain.

I had to also realize that my limbic system does not operate in time.

Even those experiences that happened decades ago, are remembered by my limbic system as if they happened yesterday. I can use words to tell myself that this was in the past, but my limbic system doesn't speak in words. It only registers experiences with no regard to how long ago they happened. So, why do I do what I don't want to do? My limbic system is full of memories that are still motivating my choices and behaviors to this day.

What is the answer to this?
The answer is what I call
THE GREAT EXCHANGE.

Clearly, my limbic system needs to experience some new positive experiences that will drive me to better choices. New positive and healthy experiences need to come into my heart to kick out the old hurtful ones. An EXCHANGE needs to take place orchestrated by the God of all comfort and heart-change.

Let me explain it another way. In working with women's groups, over and over again I try to teach them how much God loves them. How we are His children. How He cares and wants what is best for each of us. These words are powerful, but they don't negate the painful experiences that many women have faced.

I will never forget Jennifer. She so wanted to believe that God loved her, but her experience of losing her fiancé in a motorcycle accident four days before their wedding negated the words, "God loves you." The experience in her limbic system spoke louder than God's words of truth to her. She desperately wanted to receive God's love, but her experience was blocking the words. She needed an exchange of experiences.

In Romans 7:16, Paul asked another question. "Who can set me free from this?" He answers this question by saying, "Thanks be to God through Jesus Christ our Lord!"

AND? Does that really answer the question, "Who can set

me free?" YES. Jesus Christ. However, it doesn't tell us what methods He will use for this freedom to take place. What does that mean for me tomorrow when I am tempted to eat that ice cream that's in the freezer?

For many years, I took it to mean that I should pray for Jesus to do this healing for me. However, I did that, over and over again, and I still struggled with this problem. I prayed for years that Jesus Christ would remove this weight problem in my life. He had worked other miracles in my life, why not this one?

However, with this new understanding of the limbic system, I see how prayer needs to partner with God's truth – with the power of Jesus Christ – about our hearts needing to change. I needed to partner with God. It is a very important part of this healing process. Now I see. Now I understand. To explain what I finally saw, I'll take it full circle.

Jesus Christ's work on the cross cleanses and makes the beauty of GRACE available to us. It allows us to be set free. Still those are just words. They seem like "Christianese" to me when I am such a desperate failure in this area of overeating. How does Jesus do this for me when my limbic system seems to be working against me?

Here's how. Jesus is in the substitution business. He substituted His life for our sin on the cross. Once we receive Him, we begin a journey of healing. We are made more powerful in Christ as more *substitution* and *exchange* takes place to heal our limbic system.

Here's the key: The Lord wants to replace and exchange our hurtful experiences (and we all have had them) with new experiences of love and grace by putting loving, safe, and accepting people into our lives instead of more wounding relationships.

The healing that takes place in the limbic system is one of substituting experiences.
In with the new and out with the old!

That's what Jesus can and will do for you. Picture your heart full of experiences, some great and some very hurtful as is reality in this broken world. Jesus wants to replace our wounds with positive experiences.

This can start, as it did with me, with reading a book where my painful heart experiences were shared with someone bold enough to put their life in print, like I did in this book. It can start with a YouTube video, or a Christian webinar. You could be listening to a New Life Radio show and find some answers to start you on this journey. (This is a counseling show where you can call in and ask Christian counselors questions or listen – for free – to the archived shows on www.newlife.com).

You can see more about these options in the back of the book. Satan wants to make you feel that you are the only one who has experienced these hurts, but that's not true. Others have also been wounded and are willing to share their lives and their Christ-healing in so many different ways. You just need to reach out and seek, wherever you are and with however much time and resources you have. (Although many of these places are free!)

Resources! That's the key. Those who grow and start the healing process surround themselves with resources, and many are available for us. Reach out! Satan would love for you to isolate, but God has provided so many ways to have "in with the new" in your life. That's how I started my healing journey.

If you had a wounding home life, He wants to move those experiences out and to replace them with a new family of love and acceptance from the Body of Christ which can take many forms. If your marriage was painful, God knows just what you need. He is the great Healer.

Our pain started with an experience. The healing can only happen through a replacement experience – one that is safe, loving, grace-filled, and accepting. It's up to you to take the initiative to begin this searching process.

If you were in a painful relationship, then the healing has to take place with a healing relationship of love and grace. This is the GREAT EXCHANGE. I have seen this happen in our family, in my small group, in our youth group, and in our church, and in my life. It is the love of Christ at work. It is a process that begins with you asking for help! Christ is listening and knows your pain. He hears your cry for healing.

His passion for you is to replace hurtful experiences and relationships with loving ones.

When love replaces pain and woundedness, it is out with the old hurts and in with the new healing. For me, it meant that I needed to step out of the isolated and protective person that I had become and risk some new relationships. I know this can be a fearful move to make, to welcome new relationships when old ones have hurt you in the past. However, this is a necessary move for healing.

First, start with various resources that aren't too threatening (a book, a video, a large class where you can just blend in), and then you will have the courage to reach out and surround yourself with safe and loving people on a more intimate basis. I know. I did! That's how my healing all began. Jesus Christ will enable the transfer of experiences to take place, and in time your heart will be healed.

Were we originally created this way?

On my journey to understand all of this, I asked God to show me what His original intention for the limbic part of our brain was back in the Garden of Eden before the fall of man. I knew it must have had a positive purpose because we were made in His image. He showed me that it was intended to be the place of ultimate enjoyment of Him -- intimacy with Him – a place for peace and fellowship with Him. However, when the fall came and that perfect relationship with Him and our fellow man was broken, the limbic system actually started to work against us making us think it was working for us. We tried to fill that space with our own means. Jeremiah calls these "broken cisterns."

*The Lord wants to take us back to
the original state for which we were created....
to enjoy and experience Him and His love in this
experiential part of our brain and to share
that love with others.*

As He partners with us to help us experience the re-placements for our wounds, we are healed and can learn to love and pass that love on to others. These aren't just words. This can be a life-changing journey for each of us. A powerful change of heart. I am so thankful that we live in a time when God choose to reveal so much truth about recovery, healing, and our hearts.

*Understanding the limbic brain/heart
and how it works in relation to our weight issues
and eating choices is the first foundation
for change we need to embrace on this journey.*

Foundation For Change # 2
Change My Heart - Not Just My Behavior

I'm embarrassed to say that for some 55 plus years, I have been struggling with this weight issue by trying to change my behavior.   As a mature and informed Christian, I know you can tell a tree by its fruit. (Matthew 12:33) As a person thinks in their heart, so are they (Proverbs 23:7).   My outside behaviors are determined by the heart condition of my heart.

Even though I knew those truths, I prayed for years, "Lord, help me with my diet, help me not reach for food, to say no, to make better choices. Change my behavior."

I truly believed that my behavior was the problem, so I was praying for my outside behavior to change. Now I realize that this weight issue is going to continue to produce the "fruits" that it has given in the past 50 years unless I have a change of heart.

When it comes to eating, I am a child.
A child seeks to "get away with"
while an adult makes responsible choices.

Read that again!   Until I have a change of heart, I will continue to be a child and continue to try to "get away with" as much as I can. I desperately need a heart change.

I never seem to be content or satisfied. I use food instead of letting food be my fuel source. I have to "get something" from food instead of just allowing it to energize my body. These changes can't happen until I have a heart change.

Now I go around the house singing that popular song, *"Change my heart, O God. Make it ever new. Change my heart, O, God. Let me be like you."*

I see that my behavior will change as my heart changes. This realization in itself has produced the most amazing results. It has given me a calm even in the midst of a storm. Instead of feeling agitated and needing to eat, I am seeing my heart change to relax in the Lord –to be content in Him.

> *He will take care of me and help work out my issues. I don't need to numb myself and try to escape my problems. He will walk me through them.*

For this peace and contentment to happen, I need a change of heart. I can then make good decisions about my behaviors. They will be motivated not by the rod, but by the heart. I will *want to want to.* I see my changing heart (which is a process that takes time) responding to food items with an "I don't need that. I don't even want that!" Praise God, my heart is changing.

It's all a matter of focus. My prayers have now changed focus. My evaluation of myself has changed. I no longer look at my behaviors as much as my heart. How do I feel about what's going on in my life? Those feelings change as my heart changes. Am I full of peaceful faith?

This all goes back to understanding the limbic heart. My heart will change as the painful and past experiences take a hike from my heart and are replaced by new people, new attitudes towards myself, new acceptance, and new love as well as a deeper relationship with the Lord.

I now intentionally work at surrounding myself with people who can come into my heart with their love and clean me out– so to speak, replacing the hard and hurtful with the gentle and loving. Replacing the years of criticism from others with loving words from people who really do care about me. In my dedication to this book I used the expression, "When they SEE into me and like the view." That is the change of heart that can happen with the love from God's safe and caring people in my life.

We will be talking about this more and more as we get further into the book. Having a change of heart and not just behavior is a key element for change and success in the weight loss world.

I hope you start today to look not at your behaviors
but at your heart to see the changes God wants
to make –that only He can make.

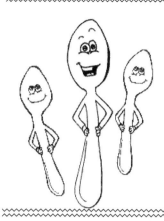

Foundation For Change # 3

Going THROUGH and not AROUND!

I love kayaking and often go out alone since my husband doesn't enjoy this sport. That's why I treasure times kayaking with my daughter. One time, we kayaked up the gorge which connects to Diablo Dam in northwest Washington state. It's a place I would never go alone.

We were told that the few boats that power up the gorge will NOT stop to help kayakers if they are in trouble unless they are imminent danger of dying. They warn you before you start on this journey to know the weather and the winds you might face.

The rocky walls of this gorge tower high above us, and there are barely any spots to pull your kayak over in case of trouble or high winds. Because of the depth of the gorge wall, shadows cause it to be harder to see the exact conditions of the water and waves. We knew all of this going in.

I have to admit, though, that with all of the cautions going into this adventure, I was a bit apprehensive. Having my wilderness-trained daughter with me helped some, but I knew if the winds came up it would be "every woman for herself!"

I could choose to stay back at the campground, or I could choose to take a risk. I knew that to reap the full joys of this experience, I had to go THROUGH the gorge.

*However, my lifestyle, with my personal
issues, shows patterns of not going
THROUGH but AROUND.*

I don't like confrontation, and I come from a family of denying avoiders. Going around an issue is the way we operate.

This really struck me when I was reviewing Psalm 23. David says, "Even if I walk THROUGH the valley of the shadow of death....I will fear no evil." THROUGH - David is challenging me to go through.

However, heading right into a storm, or into an unknown situation, is not my first choice. I always search for a way AROUND, a different path, a way to avoid, to get busy so that the problem will just go away. Over the years, food has become my first choice to take me around instead of through.

I think it is most people's natural tendency and inclination to go AROUND. However, if I had let fear take me over after hearing all of the warnings before my daughter and I headed up the thirteen mile gorge to Diablo Dam, I would have said NO. – I'm not going to put myself THROUGH that experience. Then I would have lost out on the most spectacular kayak ride of my life.

*I came out so very thankful that I had taken the
challenge to go THROUGH this scary experience.
Now I can't wait to do it again.*

As I have matured in my walk with the Lord, I see that going THROUGH is a **must** if I want to experience real transformation and freedom in my life – especially in the area of eating. I can't go around. I need to go through difficult times —face them head on – not run from relational conflicts or work challenges to the kitchen.

So here I am with this defeating eating issue. It is frankly, a valley I don't want to go THROUGH. However, after going AROUND for years, I know it is time to learn to go THROUGH.

Here's the truth: The number of times I have chosen the "route" AROUND has made a gorge, a rut, a pathway of avoidance so deep it is going to take a rescue helicopter of some type to lift me out to even be able to travel THROUGH.

Going through? I don't even know how! What would it even feel like to go through? What would be at the other end? I know what is at the end of the kitchen routine. Yummy sweets, buttery carbs – and then shame, guilt, fat, short-lived comfort, out-of control actions, needing more and more.

Watching Oprah Winfrey the other day on the Dr. Oz show after she lost 40 pounds gave me a good example how this could look. She was asked if she got stressed before doing a show. She said no, not at all.

Now she realizes it is because she "fed" her stress. She numbed her fears before going on stage. She was going AROUND instead of learning to be confident without the escape to food. Her fears were numbed by food.

I can choose to numb with food or to go THROUGH a challenging situation. Funny thing, the emotional and relational issues I was trying to avoid by going AROUND are still there waiting for me to face them – to go THROUGH them.

Actually it is not funny at all. It is very sad that being willing to go THROUGH has taken me so long to learn since the Lord promises to travel THROUGH with us and that we will "fear no evil."

What is it like going THROUGH?

It starts with one single step. One decision. Then I need to keep walking on course.   In Psalm 23, the word "walk" is a present continuous verb. We will always have to face valleys -- we will always have to do some walking THROUGH life's challenges. We might as well learn how to do it with good results and transformed maturity.

In fact, THROUGH
is the route to true joy.

Going through with the Lord does this. Going around just avoids the inevitable (and puts more pounds on our bodies!) (Book 2 - *50 Ways Out For Godly Women Who Are Overweight* gives even more examples of how I learned to go THROUGH.)

David walked through his stressful times. When he was being viciously chased by Saul to take his life,   David could have taken a side road. He had a few easy opportunities to go AROUND by killing Saul instead of going THROUGH.

One time, while Saul was relieving himself in a cave, David came upon him quite by accident. Saul was very vulnerable at that moment, and David could have easily taken his life.

However, David had learned to walk THROUGH the valleys with the Lord – that God's way THROUGH is the better way. The best things happen when we go THROUGH and not take our own routes around. God eventually took Saul's life, in His timing, in His way. David did not have his blood on his hands.

God's way THROUGH this lengthy ordeal for David was the way to prepare him to become the King. Going THROUGH accomplishes great transformation in our lives as well.

God's purposes are never wasted. His training course includes transformation and preparing for our next challenges, and it always take us THROUGH, not around.

✳ I have a choice when someone makes me upset.
I have a choice when things don't go my way.
I can go back to the old ways of kitchen trips,
or I can take a trip THROUGH
the difficulty with the Lord.

This will be a location where I will receive the Lord's comfort, wisdom, power and lessons. Going THROUGH is a place where God can do His work of transformation. It teaches us to walk more intimately with Him.

I have to say that God has made this choice very clear to me recently. I have made a list of alternatives to kitchen raiding. Take a walk (even if it is 21 degrees outside....I know how to bundle up!) - go read a book - go into a room and throw myself on the bed crying out to God about what is making me angry - call a friend - get into the car and go for a drive - go into the hot tub with my favorite verses written on 3 X 5 cards - even get my chainsaw out and start to trim trees (yes, I have my own chainsaw!) The list can go on and on.

The point is I MADE THE LIST. Now I need to MAKE THE CHOICE. I just have to walk a short distance toward my office instead of to the kitchen to read my list and make the choice to go THROUGH and not around.

Going through with the Lord is always
the way to maturity and growth.

Foundations For Change # 4

Becoming Aware!

In my close-to-50 years of walking with the Lord, I've noticed He seems to use single WORDS as a powerful way to communicate to me "the next steps" for my life. In this weight journey, two words became very significant: THROUGH (as I shared in the last foundation) and AWARE.

He is calling me to become MORE AWARE!

As much as I did not want to accept it, I was totally unaware of why I did what I did in regards to food. I didn't feel it, think about it, decide about it....I just did it. Becoming aware of my behaviors in three areas opened up an entirely new world for me as I was discovering myself on this food journey:

1. Physically   2. Emotionally, and 3. Spiritually

Physical Awareness:

Physically, I eat! I go through the motions sometimes not even realizing that I am eating and definitely not aware of how much I am eating. I'm impulsive. I get distracted easily. An idea of food comes to my mind and I fulfill it. If I have a whim that I am hungry, I get something to eat. I may not be physically hungry, but emotionally hungry – but I don't stop to become aware and to differentiate the two.

Food should satisfy, but when I am eating to satisfy an emotional hunger instead of a physical one, I will never be satisfied. It is like filling a bucket with a hole in it.

In my new awareness of my eating habits, I realized I never even took the time to physically enjoy the food. Its taste, texture, color, smell, and feel as it goes down. Food has many dimensions and as a binge eater, I just stuff it down.

Then, when I was done, I would not feel full or satisfied. I could eat a big dinner, even a Thanksgiving dinner, and leave the table still "hungry." How could this be? I scarfed it down so fast, I never stopped to enjoy each part of the meal.

I didn't even give the food time to reach the stomach, or for my body to know it had eaten anything.

The part of my body that is supposed to tell me that I have had enough has malfunctioned for years. In fact, I learned that one sign of a binge eater is eating quickly. That's been my problem for years. I race through a meal thinking about what else I can eat!

A nutritionist once told me something helpful. She said that the next time I feel hungry, put my hand over my stomach area. Then judge on a scale of one to five. Five being very physically hungry and one being very full.   Four being getting ready to need to eat and three being just ate but not yet feeling the effects of the meal.

I never wait for that to happen. Physically, this new awareness pointed me to become awake to how my body works and what it really needs. Was I hungry, emotional, just impulsively reacting to a habit, or what?

I was also not aware of how I physically looked.
I would see myself in the mirror and then like
James 1:23-24 says, "forget what I saw!"

Sometimes it takes a video or a picture of ourselves to get us to realize how out of control our physical shape has become. Awareness is the starting key to physical change.

Emotional Awareness:

For years, I never really embraced or was aware of how I felt. I stuffed my feelings because most of them I didn't want to feel. I lived in denial of my feelings. Food helped me numb those feelings.

Food made me invincible because I could just eat the feelings away and proceed on living in hurtful relation-ships and circumstances. I have learned to tolerate more than I should have!

I just never stopped long enough to feel my emotional responses to life. Keeping busy also allowed me not to feel. If I was hurt or stressed or frustrated, I would head straight to the kitchen without even thinking about it.

The urge to make a batch of chocolate chip cookies just "came upon me." Or I'd say, "I'm in the mood for some cherry pie!" It wasn't just when I was upset, either. Sometimes my actions had no real conscious reason.

I could be happy and head for the kitchen!
My habits responded to any kind of emotion.
Celebrate, pain, or escape.

The Feelings Discovery Chart, an idea originally presented to me by Christian marriage counselors Milan and Kay Yerkovich, has helped bring my feelings to the forefront for me. Their chart is called *Soul Words*. The chart I put together is below. (There is also a larger version on my web page: www.freshlookthinking.com).

It is a great tool to help me know how I am feeling, and even helps my family members. My husband and I will use this chart to prompt communication on an emotional level when we are going through some difficult decisions or experiences.

Now I use this chart on a regular basis as I continue my journey into my emotions. When I am about to go into some challenging or difficult experience, I get the *Feelings Discovery Chart* out and circle the words I am feeling. When I have just experienced something hurtful or am in the middle of a relationship conflict, I pull out the list and journal my feelings.

I suggest you circle all of the feelings that resonate in your heart right now. Some can fit into several categories. Even if you are feeling low, be sure to consider some positive feelings, also.

You will probably want to make copies of this to have for use during your week. This chart has been a huge help in defining how I felt. That was the first step before deciding what actions I should take in certain situations.

Now I am more aware of my feelings and
this helps me do something besides
GO TO THE KITCHEN.

I am no longer just afraid or angry. I can pick specific words that pinpoint more clearly how I am feeling. Now I can feel baffled, marginalized, betrayed, or disrespected, not just upset in a vague sort of way.

You will see from the list there is such a variety of emotions we can feel, and that this list serves us by helping us get in touch with our emotions and then to more deeply understand others as well. Counselors who use this tool note that just bringing the feelings your are experiencing into the light is a huge part of the healing process.

Feelings Discovery Chart

POSITIVE FEELINGS	grateful	encouraged	optimistic	relieved
delighted	ecstatic	overjoyed	happy	floating
content	satisfied	standing firm	content	peaceful
MOTIVATED FEELINGS	driven and determined	self-pity and comparing	risk-taking/ brave	non-stop talking
hopeful	nervous	positive	thrilled	focused
high-energy	enthusiastic	giddy	reignited	excited
Passionate	Self-confident	fearful/ worried	confident	bewildered
exhausted	depressed	disappointed	confused	perplexed
skeptical	despairing	curious	creative	disciplined
organized	enlightened	restless	assertive	frozen
overwhelmed	beaten down	indifferent	bored	planning
RELATIONAL FEELINGS	refreshed love	rejoicing in change	desiring to know & listen	secure and protected

connected	comforted	injured	angry/ furious	forgiving
deserted	romantic	appreciative	trusting	tenderness
wounded	rejected	owned/slave	annoyed	isolated
isolated	insecure	inconsiderate	tolerated	invisible
betrayed	unwanted	disconnected	private	ignored
WOUNDED FEELINGS	ridiculed	marginalized not valuable	mocked and teased	allowed no voice
shamed	tolerated	despised	stupid	ashamed
forgotten	invisible	violated	abandoned	unwanted
rejected	over-looked	let down	distrust	suspicion
put-down	hated	humiliation	exposed	grieved
traumatized	deceived	sad	unlovable	worthless

While this chart will not fit on one page, there is a one-page document on my web page at **www.FreshLookThinking.com**

Recently, I had an amazing realization. I began thinking about a very painful and shocking experience that I had gone through in the past. I have studied the stages of grief most people go through when they have experienced a great loss. Psychologist say that first, we feel numb and in shock.

Then we begin to deny. After this, we get angry. Finally, we are willing to accept and adjust to our new reality.

It shocked me to realize that I my journeys through these stages totally avoided the emotionally angry stage. I went from being in shock to denial and then jumped to acceptance, doing so in a very raw "that's the way life is" sort of way.

I never got angry,
and that's not healthy.

God got angry. It is a very legitimate and necessary emotion to heal our woundedness. Our anger helps to define us.

Christian counselor Dr. Dave Stoup, who is on the radio program New Life Live, helps women in his counseling office go into grief when they have been abandoned or betrayed, but he notes he has a hard time getting them to feel angry. It is like Christian women were taught they don't have a right to be angry. We have been trained that is not a Christian thing to do.

I was talking with a girlfriend who just discovered that her husband had lied to her about having affairs for years. She couldn't get angry. I told her, "that makes me angry that all of these years he has blamed the problems in your marriage on you while at the same time he has been lying and having multiple affairs."

I asked her, "Doesn't that make you angry?" It didn't. In her mind, a good Christian wife no matter how betrayed, does not have the right to be angry. Love does not allow anger in her thinking. Some feel the anger would serve no purpose. However, feeling those feelings is a huge part of our healing.

I was afraid of anger. I was afraid that I might lose more if I was angry over a situation. Now I am aware of my anger and if it is righteous or self-centered. James 1:20 says that *"Man's anger is never a way to achieve God's righteousness."*

I needed to see how feeling God's anger, not man's anger, could be a healthy part of my healing – especially in my relationship to food.

God showed me that part of my healing
in the area of eating was my need
to become aware of my feelings.

I have discovered that I, the queen of denial, used to jump into the raw acceptance of life, and in the process, I lost my ability to feel, often becoming quick to freeze in a situation. This has not served me well. Now I am "feeling aware!"

My feelings don't rule me, but being aware of them has helped me understand myself and wisely respond to my situations. It has also made me more compassionate to others.

There is one more area of awareness:

Spiritual Awareness:

When Jesus died and rose, and then ascended, He told the disciples that the Father was going to send the Holy Spirit to be with them and to guide them. This Holy Spirit is present in our lives if we have received Jesus Christ as Savior and Lord.

One important quality of the Holy Spirit is that He is the great comforter. Since we use food as an emotional *comfort* and that hasn't worked well for us, we need to learn how to turn to the Holy Spirit as a comforter.

One Christian author noted that when he turned to the Holy Spirit for comfort, within five minutes of asking he will be overwhelmed with His comfort. Why doesn't this happen to me? Well, I admit, I just don't wait the five minutes. It only takes me one minute to move towards the kitchen for food comfort.

However, when we are done bingeing, the problem area in which we needed comfort still exists. We have accomplished nothing – just delayed the inevitable.

The Holy Spirit delights to meet our needs for comfort. However, He is spiritual and food is material. There needs to be a spiritual awareness of what is different between these two types of comfort.

Food is something I can hold. It is a rapid comforter, but can't offer long-lasting comfort. It is a pseudo-comfort. When all is said and done, it is actually an idol we worship if I am depending upon something like food to meet my needs or to dull my pain instead of calling upon God to help.

The Holy Spirit is ready to come to our aid in any way necessary. To tell us what to say, to offer comfort for our feelings, to guide us into our next appropriate step. He is all we need.   However, spiritual things are so much harder to grasp than material things. Cake with icing is here, now, touchable, smellable. Immediate.

The Holy Spirit offers His own version of comfort. Becoming aware of how the Spirit works is a maturing skill. It requires stopping, asking, waiting, and then watching for God to work. Aware that HE *will* respond. Aware that the minute we pray He sets into motion to answer our prayers.   We just don't wait. (Sometimes, we also have a need to confess a sin to remove any barrier to be able to receive from the Lord.)

We don't have the patience to learn how the Holy Spirit generously meets our needs, and this is probably the greatest area we all need to become aware of in this challenge of weight control.

Substituting the spiritual for the material means allowing the spiritual power of God to fill those painful areas of our lives instead of using food and material possessions, activities, or inappropriate relationships to try to fill the holes in our soul.

At first, it was hard to "see" this substitution since the material and the spiritual are so different. I learned I couldn't have expectations of how the Spirit of God would meet my needs. I also couldn't define what that comfort should look like. I needed to be open to His ways even though they were new to me and very different. Now I see how much better they are.

When my husband and I were first married, we had some conflicts around Christmas presents. My husband would always go out and buy whatever he needed. He never had a Christmas list that we could have to joyfully buy something for him. It just wasn't the way his family celebrated the holiday. He's much better now, but I often equate this to not waiting for the Holy Spirit to give comfort. He couldn't wait for us to bless him with a gift.

> *God created us. He knows us.*
> *He knows every wound, hurt, scare*
> *and empty spot.*
> *He also knows how to fill them with powers*
> *and comforts that don't require chewing.*
> *Chew on that for a while.*

Foundations
For Change # 5
Call It What It Is!

"A problem well-stated is a problem half-solved." That's one of my mottos. Sounds good, doesn't it? Call a problem a problem . My problem, however, was I didn't recognize problems to begin the work to solve them.

I've experienced much of life with my head buried in the sand like an ostrich going through the motions of life – numbing with food. I just read a new expression from Henry Cloud that makes a lot of sense to me.

"Wise people have problems.
Foolish people have patterns."

OUCH! I want to be wise, but I have a few patterns that need breaking. It's like I don't see the red light on my car's dash flashing "Oil Needed!" I'm blind to the fact that my child is having a difficult time, or that my husband is frustrated, or about how I feel with what's going on in my life. I just travel along trying to keep life on an even keel.

They nicknamed me Mrs. Fix-it, but I never fixed anything. I ignored it all and hoped it would go away. That was my way of fixing things.

It's easy to think, if you ignore it long enough, the problem really isn't there! It's the ignored elephant in the room syndrome.

As I shared, *awareness* was a skill I had to learn. It meant becoming *aware* of my responses, peoples' responses to my responses or words, my feelings, other's feelings, to behaviors that were a bit odd.

I remember one time a friend observed something going on in our family and said, "You know that is not normal, not healthy, don't you?" Actually, I didn't. I didn't actually "see" anything. I just went about life.

Now I see my denial was more of a cover-up. I really believed that if I ignored negative behavior it was a way to demonstrate love to another person, or so I thought. Yes, now I know that's enabling. I didn't call a problem a problem.

When God pointed out to me that I needed to *stop and look around*, an entire new world opened up to me. I needed to notice my behaviors – when and why I reacted as I did.

Most of all, I needed to feel my feelings and state the problem.

I began to see that when "THIS" happened, "THAT" was my typical response. When a harsh word came from my husband – to the kitchen I went. When I couldn't fix my children – a trip to the refrigerator was unconsciously made. If a friend hurt me in some way – to the cookie jar with me! Honest *awareness* began the healing process. I was then able to name the problem.

My husband and I met with a very astute nutritionist one time. Her advice to us was to write down everything that went into our mouths. That means we had to be *aware* of our eating patterns. Exactly!

She noted that most people aren't even aware of what they are eating, how much, when, why and how. They don't see the problem. Thus they can't state the problem.

During this awakening to call a problem a problem, I noticed how God helped His people define their problems clearly. For example, God asked Moses and the Israelites, "Where are your gods? In whom do you take refuge? God wanted to help them define their behaviors.

Once they identified their idols, God said, "Okay, let *these* help you....hide in *these*." What is *these?* Their idols. Jeremiah asked the same question to the people of his time. (Jeremiah 2:28 and Deuteronomy 32:38)

Something besides the Lord God had become their god. Do you know what that something was? It was what they were eating and their love of it. He wanted them to call it what it was: Idolatry. Loving something more than God. He wanted them to be aware there was a problem!

In Hosea, God notes that they
"loved their raisin cakes." (Hosea 3:1, NIV)

My girlfriend and I have a "code" when we have been off course in our eating. We'll say, "I loved my raisin cakes today."

Jesus tells us that He came to help the sick. Only the sick need a physician. However, if we are not *aware* that we are sick and in need of healing, He can't begin the work in our hearts that He wants to do. We need to define our eating as gluttony, selfishness, walking out of the Spirit, whatever form it takes.

In other words, call sin, sin.
Then, what do we need to do when we sin?
I John 1:9 tells us we need to confess it!
If we don't call sin, sin, we won't move into confession.

However, after years of this sin being repeated, I have to admit that I've gotten rather tired confessing again and again. God, however, never gets tired of us taking steps towards him in honesty and confession. Call it what it is. SIN. Confess it for what it is! SIN.

Now realize, when we become aware of how "eating our raisin cakes" is sin to us, our response should never take the form of condemnation at the end of the day.

Often I find myself judging my day by what I ate. Who I was became what I had eaten that day! Instead, how about asking how I loved others that day? No, even though that is God's standard for how the day went, my evaluation of myself and my day revolved more around how successful my diet went that day – not how I loved others.

James 4:17 tells us that *"If a woman knows to do right and does not do it, to that woman it is sin."* (*Change of gender is mine.*) I needed to call sin, sin. To call idolatry, idolatry. However, I learned it doesn't mean I need to take a trip down wallowing-in-self-pity lane.

No! Jesus came to earth and provided for our sin. God tells us in I John 1:9, "If we confess our sins, He is faithful and just. He forgives, and He cleanses us from our sins." That is a powerful verse. I noticed that my only responsibility is to call sin sin, and then confess it to the Lord.

The Lord then is responsible to forgive, decide upon the just response for me and then to cleanse me from this sin. Honestly, I get so tired of confessing over and over again the same sin.

Confession, though, is the plan God worked out for us in Jesus. The process of cleansing from that habit of sin does not begin until we are *aware* of our sin *and* confess it.

Awareness, acknowledging, not denying, calling it what it is — stating the problem – all leads to the next steps towards healing which God wants to work in our lives. Satan would love to get you to believe that because this battle is ongoing and not quickly solved, that God's power and plan are not "working."

The devil is a liar. Let God be true!
Work the plan!

A huge part of my transformation began with awareness of my sin patterns, my responses, my cover-ups, my reactions, my habits, and my denial. This included honest conversations with God daily (or hourly) that contain no condemnation, but lots of awareness of sin and confession. His hope for us comes in the form of encouragement that healing is on its way, and the starting button is our confession when we call gluttony sin.

Call it what it is! SIN! Confess it!
Then you will see God's power invade your life.
When pride keeps you from confession,
no progress will be made!

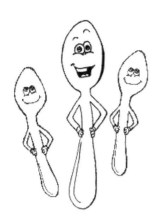

Foundation For Change # 6

Identify Unreal Expectations

Over the years in my walk with the Lord, I have noticed how He has "moved me" along. I identified three progressive steps to maturity that were needed to really begin to embrace the fullness of Christ in my life.

Dealing with my
UNREALISTIC EXPECTATIONS
was number one.

I pictured everything and then expected life to go as I pictured it. From a new job to raising kids to married life – I have expectations of what *should* be. However, life just doesn't turn out the way we expected.

I love asking women when I speak, "Did your life turn out the way you expected?" The answer is always a resounding "NO!" However, at one small group I was leading, two new gals attended. I asked the group, "Did your life turn out the way you expected?" They immediately answered, "YES!" I was taken aback for a moment. Really? They said, "Yes, we expected it to be awful and it was!"

Oh dear. Most women have expectations in their lives, and some are okay, but it is the unreal ones that get us down. I see this is especially true when I go on a new diet. I EXPECT to lose lots of weight in a short time...AMEN!! However, it really never happens that way. My expectation is just too vigorous and unrealistic. It is unsustainable. My EXPECTATIONS are just unrealistic and even unhealthy.

When I step on the scale, I EXPECT to see a lower number. I expect to lose and not gain. How quickly I forgot that I really didn't eat well the day before weighing in. However, I still EXPECT the best.

In my spiritual journey, the second step for me was SURVIVAL.

After I saw that my expectations were not being met, I went into survival mode where I began to manipulate my life to be what I want it to be. I manipulated people, circumstances, and myself to measure up to what I expected.

This went on for years, and was quite a struggle. It included expectations for my kids and my husband, none of which was welcomed eagerly by them. You can imagine! It also included crazy fad diets to make the weight loss be what I wanted it to be. I worked so hard to make things happen.

Then someone asked me the Dr. Phil question: *"How is that working for you?"* In all honesty, I had to admit that it wasn't. None of my manipulations worked to a positive end.

That's when I moved into the third stage in my spiritual walk: THE DISCOVERY STAGE.

God wanted me to discover His ways and His plans and His timing. What a contrast! Relax and discover. Take one day at a time. No race to the finish. Just trust and obey. In this process, God helped me discover the sane thing to do in regards to eating. First, diets don't work. Having a sane and healthy eating plan does.

Not setting a goal to lose 30 pounds in one month, but maybe five pounds a month was a more realistic expectation. Then, adopting a new way of healthy eating, instead of deprivation and rigid legalism. Life lived in reality –walking in the Spirit. Not denying yourself healthy items and not living on 400 calories a day. Not to take up the world's ways of legalistic diets.

God makes it very clear,
"Seek Him first."
Then you can expect that
"all of these things will be taken care of!"
(Matthew 6:33)

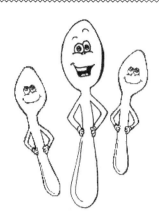

Foundation For Change # 7

Say It Out Loud!

In any given moment, I have a lot of thoughts running through my mind. If my husband asks, "Penny for your thoughts," I usually tell him they are worth at least a quarter.

Christian speaker, Mark Gungor, presents a seminar he calls, "*Laugh Your Way to A Better Marriage.*" In a talk he entitled "*Two Brains,*" he compares the male and female brain. He describes males as having a one-thought-at-a-time brain. Women, however, are like electrical storms in their brain. Hundreds of thoughts are sparking their wiring at lightning speed.

My husband laughed so hard when he heard that. It perfectly described my brain – always in motion!

Some of these thoughts are better left unsaid, but others need to be communicated – especially when I am being tempted. Calling out like Jesus did in Luke 4 when he was in the wilderness being tempted by Satan has been a great example to me.

One of the greatest lessons I learned about Satan involves what he has access to and what limits he has. I learned that while he can PUT ideas into my mind, he can't READ my mind. He does, however, observe my behavior. What I do indicates a lot to him about what I am thinking.

Handling temptation really changed for me when I learned I needed to say my rebuke to Satan out loud.

Do you realize how significant this is to our resisting the devil? He is often very observant if I am tired, hungry, discouraged, lonely, or angry. He left Jesus in the wilderness promising to come back at a "more opportune time."

I have lots of "opportune times" in my average day for Satan to tempt me. One day I saw how this works. I walked into the kitchen and smelled that beautiful aroma of freshly made cookies. Yes, my older daughter has just baked some chocolate chip cookies. Oh, dear! The smell is enough to lure you in!

I had just started a diet and of course it wasn't a chocolate chip cookie diet, so they were off limits to me. However, Satan used his scheme against me and told me (speaking into my mind), *"YOU WANT A COOKIE."*

When these thoughts came into my mind (remember, Satan has the power to put thoughts into our minds), I said to myself, "No, I don't. I'm on a diet, and I'm not going to spoil it."

Once again – no actually about four times – Satan repeated himself. *"You want a cookie."* I kept combating him in my mind, *NO, I don't!* His tempting words, though, didn't stop.

Then I remembered. I needed to say those words out loud. Satan wasn't hearing my refusals. He can't read my mind. He did, however, observe my behavior which included a longing look in the direction of the cookies and a whispered comment, "Those smell good!" With those cues, which told him that I was in a vulnerable state, he wasn't going to stop his tormenting suggestions.

It was then that I said out loud, emphatically and with frustration (since I felt that I had told him already enough times),

"No, I don't want a cookie. Get behind me Satan!"

That took care of it. I spoke out loud like Jesus did and Satan fled the scene. However, my out loud words posed another problem. I didn't realize that my younger daughter (about 10 at the time) had brought a friend home with her. I had never met this new friend.

They were sitting on the other side of the three-quarter wall that backed up to the kitchen. My daughter was showing her family photo albums, and they were giggling up a storm. When I spoke out, "Satan get behind me. I don't want a cookie," the visitor asked my daughter, "Who's that? What's that all about?" My daughter turned to her matter-of-factly and said, *"Oh, that's just my mom telling Satan to bug off."*

I treasure that story because it means I had taught my daughter well the importance of speaking out loud in a temptation situation. It also served to remind me to practice what I am teaching my kids. Say it out loud.

Temptation comes up out of the blue. That's the danger of it. We never know when to expect it. We need to be ready to speak out loud our rebukes to Satan's ploys.

Temptations come from our flesh according to James 4:2. James, the brother of Jesus, notes that our temptations arise from "conflicting passions within ourselves." You know I really DID want a cookie. There's no doubting that. There was a conflicting passion within me. I wanted it, but at the same time I didn't want it.

In this case, I wanted to be healthy and fit more than I wanted the cookie. (At least at that moment! – There have been other moments where my choices have not been as good.)

Satan (and/or his gluttony demons) is right there to do what Jesus warned us about – "to steal, kill, and destroy" (John 10:10). He wants to steal my resolve, to kill my body with unhealthy binges, and to destroy my intimate walk with the Lord.

He wants to get me off course focusing on the flesh instead of the spirit.

I need to be ready at any time to refute, defy,
and expose his schemes to the power
of the Holy Spirit by speaking out loud.

Satan can even hear a whisper, he just doesn't have the power to read our minds. I thank the Lord, He can read my mind and heart, but Satan can't.

Wrapping Up
The Foundations for Change

I've still got a lot of living and learning to do with the Lord, but so far these are the seven foundations that I have found to be KEY to gaining success in this eating dilemma.

In Review:

1. *Understand how your Limbic Brain/Heart works. It wants to repeat behaviors that bring pleasure and comfort, such as food. God wants to transform our limbic heart to be full of His love.*

2. *Realize we need to focus on God changing our hearts before we can see our behavior change. This is our number one prayer.*

3. *We need to go THROUGH our challenges in life instead of going AROUND them by numbing ourselves with food.*

4. *Be sure to be AWARE of Spiritual, Physical and Emotional conditions in our personal realities. Learn not to live in denial.*

5. *Call it what it is - sin! Sin calls for confession, which sets in motion God's power in our life.*

6. *Don't expect unrealistic results. We are looking for a life-time of change, not a quick fix.*

7. *Fight temptations out loud! Satan can't hear your thoughts. Just like Jesus, we need to declare out loud our rebukes to Satan.*

Section Two

Twenty-One Myths We "Feed" Ourselves

Satan is a liar, the accuser of Christians, and unfortunately we have bought into his lies. Here are some common myths or lies that are used to defeat us.

Myth # 1

I've tried everything!!

"*Enemy on the starboard, coming in quickly!*"

"*I see them, Captain! They're as good as gone, Sir! I'll give them the* **whole nine yards***!*"

The other day my husband was retelling a story to me which involved some World War II fighter airplanes. Mounted on the wings of these planes were machine guns. When the pilot saw an enemy plane, he would alert the gunner who proceeded to shoot them down. Then he'd say to the Captain, "We got 'em. I gave 'em the whole nine yards!"

The whole nine yards? Believe it or not, that now-popular phrase came from the ammunition used with machine guns on fighter planes. The oval-shaped belt holding a row of bullets set in a machine gun belt is exactly nine yards long (27 feet), and that's where the expression originated. The bullets were rapidly fired from the machine gun as the nine-yard belt traveled through the gun.

***When you fired the "whole nine yards"
it meant you had given the enemy
everything you had.***

How often I have thought to myself, *I have given this dieting thing the whole nine yards! I have tried every diet under the sun and nothing works. I have exhausted every possible remedy and program!*

How easily I took on the "whole nine yards" mentality. Yet, in reality, I had not given the entire "nine yards" to any of my efforts. In fact, I have probably only given two yards if I am really honest with myself. I'm so unrealistic about my efforts, and to be honest, I usually get hopeless before all nine yards had been fired at my problem.

I had to accept that my crazy eating patterns took years to develop, so it wasn't going to be any quick fix. It is going to take more time and more work than I seemed to be willing to give. I never "fired off" enough rounds. I never gave the "whole nine yards" of effort – and then some - to defeat this enemy.

Oh, I made plans, all right. I even wrote them down on paper, bought a notebook to monitor my efforts, resisted going to certain restaurants, and even attended meetings thinking the entire time that surely that has got to be at least nine yards of effort.

One by one, I'd convince myself that the newest diet, the newest plan, the newest idea just didn't work. It was the program's fault, certainly not my fault. Then I saw this expression:

Plan your work,
and work your plan.

In all honesty, I planned. Oh, I'm very good at getting excited about new ideas, new plans, new systems. I just never WORKED the plan! After a few failures, I would start saying, "That diet just doesn't work."

I'd convince myself that I had given it everything I had – the "whole nine yards." Who was I fooling? In so many cases, I wilted like a plant that hasn't been watered for weeks. My resolve, my determination, my enthusiasm saying that this time it was going to be better quickly disintegrated!

When the truth is revealed, I really don't WORK THE PLAN.
I give it more excuses than work.

I'm usually not a wimp when it comes to hard work, but in this area I seem to be so easily defeated. I give up before I even start. The old enemy patterns defeat me every time.

This realization was the first step to really beginning to give my plans the "whole nine yards." Most plans WILL work. I just don't WORK them hard enough.

The second step became clear to me when I admitted I was stuck - defeated - feeling hopeless. I couldn't give it the whole nine yards. I was deflated! I had lost motivations.

That's when I attended (via computer) an amazing LIFE COACHING webinar through Henry Cloud and John Townsend. (www.cloudtownsend.com) They invite people like me who are stuck to watch a webinar each month to get ideas from their great leadership skills on how to energize goals.

No matter what goals you have for your life, these ideas are a breath of fresh air to getting unstuck. I not only "attended" the webinar faithfully each month, but I invited a few others to join me in a goal setting group which also met monthly. This was re-commended by the leaders.

I would share with the gals in this new group the ideas from the webinar that John and Henry shared each month. We came to call this group "3G" - Goals, Growth, Group. It is now our fourth year, and we still meet to encourage one another in our goals. At the end of the year, we have a retreat together to celebrate all that God has done over the year in our lives. We were all amazed at the fruit we produced by working the truths we learned. We helped each other to achieve the "whole nine yards."

This group came to mean so much to me, and I'm sure the others would agree. Everyone had/has different goals from writing a book – to starting a company – to improving a marriage – to cleaning up clutter in their homes – to developing their leadership skills – to living within a budget - to developing better relationships with their kids - to healing from cancer....and even to lose weight.

> *There is a big difference between setting*
> *goals for yourself with yourself*
> *– and setting goals with others*
> *who can offer encouragement and ideas.*

In the webinar, we learned that people are a necessary and a wonderful source of energy for goals to be accomplished and change to take place in our lives. Others are a part of the whole nine yards. In fact, we aren't working the plan efficiently if we don't include others.

Take a second and hold up your thumb and fingers in the shape of an "0." Then open it up so that it makes a "C" instead. There is the difference. Henry Cloud calls it a "closed system" ("0" shape where nothing can get in) or an "open system" (a "C" shape open to new ideas.)

We need to be open to gaining from others to make the entire nine yards work. People can be energy to us, as Henry

Cloud explains beautifully in his book *The Power of the Other*.

> *One of the first things I learned about getting*
> *unstuck is that I needed to be open*
> *to people feeding into my lives.*

I needed to be open to new ideas, to ask questions, to receive ideas, to actually look for help, to admit my need, and to try their suggestions without a bunch of "but, but, but, that will never work" – or my famous phrase, "tried that before."

Now before you read this thinking that this is just an accountability program, let me set the record straight. I really don't think that many of us know what accountability really means. One time, in my naive fashion, I asked one of my really good friends to be my weight-loss accountability partner. She turned me down flat. She said she didn't want it to ruin our friendship. She was so wise. She told me, "I will never get between a woman and her food. It's as dangerous as getting between a mother bear and her cubs."

Now I have a better idea about what accountability means, and I admit that it is now a wonderful part of my life. For example, when you come along side someone who is struggling with eating issues, weight shouldn't be the only focus.

Why are they eating their way into pain? I had to realize that weight isn't really my issue. It is only a symptom. So many issues like those mentioned in Section 1 on the Foundations for Change are key.

So why are we trying to eat our way out of pain?

Henry Cloud tells a story about a CEO who was gaining a tremendous amount of weight each month. The men who worked with him were concerned, so they set up an accountability program. They met with him once a week to check to see how he was doing. He wasn't doing well at all. In fact, he continued to gain weight in spite of their efforts to hold him accountable. (In fact, Henry suggested they quit meeting with him as they might kill him with their "help" if this continued!)

Again, weight was not the real issue, but in these once a week meetings they didn't address anything but his weight. What was motivating the weight gain? This CEO wasn't even aware of why he couldn't get a handle on this problem. When it all came out in the open, he and his friends came to realize that there were some specific issues which were motivating his out-of-control eating.

First, they realized he had experienced quite a few deaths in his family in the recent past, and no one had walked him through the grieving process. It happened during a busy time of taking on this new CEO position, so he just moved on without any emotional acknowledgment of these losses in his life.

When that happens, we are actually burying the hurt alive. That's when we begin to eat from the inside out!

The other thing that came to light was his need for more training in his new job. He was feeling overwhelmed and even inadequate in taking on this new CEO position. He didn't want to admit this to anyone, so he just did his best and took his stress with him to the refrigerator. The company realized that he was a good man for this position, they just needed to invest in some training in the areas where he felt he had gaps.

Within a little over a year, he had lost his excess weight and was in control of his whims to overeat. Accountability to him became more than just a "hall monitor" watching his every step.

It became a group of people coming along side of him in love to walk him through his realities – his under-the-surface needs.

They got to know the person
instead of just the problem.

Giving the whole nine yards to me now means asking the tough questions. *Why do I overeat anyway?* It also gets rid of the excuses that I gave for so long. Then you can give the "whole nine yards" to the real issues instead of just excuses.

Myth # 2

I just need a good diet, and I'll lose the weight.

When my youngest daughter graduated from college, I lost a lot of weight through the a certain diet program. It cost a lot of money, and I gained all the weight back. – and then some. (In fact, that is what the studies show – that we tend to gain more back than we lose after we end a diet). Ouch! All that sacrifice, cost, and hard work for what – more weight gain.

Then, for close to two years, I went on another type of diet plan. It didn't cost a lot of money, and it really worked for me, but – you guessed it – I gained it all back. Parts of the diet were just too hard to maintain for long periods of time. I couldn't handle not having some fruit in my diet, and I am not a big vegetable eater!

Life was then lived with no diet. No constraints. Hopelessness. Fear of the scale. No discipline. Out from under the strict discipline that diets bring, I was a free soul – or so I thought.

However, the pounds continued to rise at the same speed as my guilt and embarrassment. I realized that I do with eating like I did with talking, at least according to my mom. I speak before thinking and I eat before thinking. Into the mouth it goes – no thought, plan, or consideration!

Health-wise, weight-wise, I was buying into the lie of *The Standard American Diet* (SAD as I now call it!). The potato chips – because you can't have a sandwich without chips. The cookies – because you can't have a meal without a sweet dessert. The sweets – the fried foods – the larger and larger portions -- all American traditions.

I attended a conference with several people from foreign countries. They couldn't believe the portion sizes of dinners and lunches served at the conference center. They left half on their plates which made an impression on me.

A few years back, I did a study where I wrote down everything I ate. At the end of the week I evaluated. Much to my shock and chagrin, this exercise revealed that I was a processed food junkie!! Working full time and having a busy life-style can do that to you. Fast food, packaged foods, pre-made foods. Oh, the salt and sugar and the unknowns!

When I eventually had to go into the "saved for such a day" bag of clothes that were too big in the past just so I had something to wear, I knew it was time to do something.

To be honest, I don't want to diet!! Does anyone? In this area, my middle name is "rebellion!"

I just needed a good diet. That's what I kept telling myself. There are new ones coming out all of the time. I should be able to find one. However, I knew I would also need to psyche up. The idea of even going on another diet slayed me. Then I learned a blatant truth. No diet will work for the long term. When we diet, it is based laws and laws defeat.

Romans 7:5 tells us, "The law stimulated our sinful passions."

(Phillips translation) We want what is forbidden. Deprivation tends to do that. Diets don't work.

However, we do need a plan
– a life-long heart-changed attitude
towards food and a plan for healthy eating.

Okay, I told myself, *so this time would not be a diet.* This *time would be a resolution to walk more closely with the Lord, to let Him change my heart, and to involve others in this process of change.*

I know I am serious when I mark it on my already very full calendar. (Leadership coaches call this "Calendaring It!") My plan: *In two weeks...on a Monday..... followed by a weight program starting at the local church on Wednesday ....YES, that's my target.*

I have to admit, I had no determination. Just a date marked on the calendar. The only hope I relied upon were my prayers that God would fill my heart with motivation and determination by that Monday.

I also prayed for a plan, not a diet, but a healthy plan that would work for my likes and dislikes. During this two week "psych up" period of time, I found out about a new healthy eating plan that had elements for losing weight and elements for maintaining. It offered healthy options. It included high protein/low carbs, a variety of healthy foods I like, allowed for choices, offered a grocery list, and gave several recipe options.

I felt it was a gift from God for me. There are quite a few plans like this available. I just had to commit to lose the weight slowly and not to be "on a diet" with high expectations for rapid change. I needed to give God the time to allow my heart to be changed and to adopt a life-long lifestyle. I'd call this learning to rest in Him.

I knew I needed a plan to start because I don't do well with freedom. I had just proven that. Freedom to me moves quickly into slavery. You may have heard the expression, "The good news is, we have a free will. The bad news is we have a free will!"

My free will takes me places I shouldn't go --to a whole package of cookies, three bowls of ice cream, and the list could go on and on!!! It's that rebellion thing in me.

I am pleased to report that God showed up on that Monday with a great supply of determination. I was able to follow the plan. You have to realize what I am fighting in this – a life time pattern of failure. Plans last for a while, and then my will power gives out. I needed God's determination planted in me because my will power is "ill power!" He was changing my heart to embrace this plan.

That prayer began a process – the process of reality in life, which includes success and failure, growth and heart-changes. All of this takes time and intentionality.

The key is to realize that diets don't work.
Never will, never have.
What you lose you gain back and more.

I've learned that instead of a diet, I needed a realistic plan to slowly lose and to maintain that loss while learning a new way of life. I am seeing my heart change, my choices change, and my victories grow. No process or change is straight uphill. There are dips and snags along the way. (Oh, yes there are!)

I try to get right back on course when
(not if) there is a failure.

This is probably because our eating habits are so tied into our moods, our relationships to others, and to how we handle success and failure –and to our motivating limbic system.

It is no longer my goal to lose the weight quickly. It has to become a way of life – a focus on the change of heart and the transformation of my limbic system. I can't show you before and after photos because my after is still in the making.

God has provided us with so many wonderful healthy foods. I am going to eat the foods the Lord has given us as fresh, pure, tasty, and ready to supply the needs of my body.

God told us that every good gift from above is good, and meant to be gratefully received (James 1:17). He has provided so many gifts from above – garden foods, spices, meats, eggs, and so many others. So – Apples- YES. Various fruits- YES. Grass-fed beef and chicken with no chemical alterations (hard to find and more expensive, but worth it!) -YES. Eggs- YES. God made these things. They are gifts to us. My goal is to make a commitment to eat those first and foremost.

I found that there is a big difference between 100 calories of green beans and 100 calories of chocolate cookies.

While calories essentially do count, it is more the type of calories that count even more. I'm working on this as a focus, and am moving in a more healthy way.

Soda is maybe one of the worst culprits. In our family, we have tried to eliminate soda and have replaced it with water. That was HUGE in our family, and it was HUGE for our health. We felt the difference in just a few weeks.

Don't let me make you think that I am now this perfect health food nut. That is far from the truth. I am just leaning in that direction more and more. As my heart changes, my food choices change. I'd like to see 90% of my diet be wholesome unprocessed foods instead of the 20% it was before. Change is gradual. Diets make us think of swift change. Changing our way of life takes time, focus, and commitment to the value in all of this.

I decided to call my plan
"GETTING FUELED."
That is the purpose of food, after all
– to fuel our bodies to obtain peak performance.
It is not going to be a diet plan
because diets fail.

Myth # 3

I really don't eat that much!

How many times have you heard from others or said yourself, "I don't understand how I can gain weight so easily. I really don't eat that much!"

I decided to test this out in myself. I kept a record of what went into my mouth for two weeks. That isn't a very long period of time, but it was long enough to reveal a few startling truths about ME – significant truths I had failed to see!

First, I noticed my portions! OUCH! I really DID eat THAT much! I had been deceiving myself. That had to change with smaller bowls and plates – and putting some part of what I dished up back into the serving bowl.

Sometimes we don't realize how much we eat throughout the day, maybe not at one meal, but the number of snacks have to be added in there. Sugary drinks have to also be included.

Second, to reiterate what I just shared in Myth 2, I also noticed WHAT was going into my mouth. I saw I ate about one to two "God made" foods in a day, or some days I ate all processed foods with no fresh fruit or vegetables. My diet was way over the top with the SAD foods (Standard American Diet). Easy, time-efficient, yet imbalanced. I knew that had to change.

I sat down and made a list of what God made. Then I planned an eating routine around these items first. That evolved into a huge change for me.

I had to become aware of what was
going into my mouth and the amount - now
with an emphasis on moderation and whole foods.

Then, ***third***, I noticed that I didn't have any regular eating time plan. I was all over the clock. I ate when I f*elt* like it. It wasn't based on hunger or even the need to eat. I never stopped to THINK about what was going into my mouth and when. Half hour before dinner – a snack. Snacking and nibbling while fixing dinner. A walk through the kitchen and of course, I had to grab a snack. That, too, had to stop. I needed to become AWARE.

Now my plan includes a 12-hour fast overnight. Whatever time I stop eating in the evening, I can't eat breakfast until that time the next morning – 12 hours later. There have been so many times I wanted a snack, but then resisted because it was late and that meant I would have to postpone breakfast for hours.

I always eat breakfast as that is also recommended. It tells your body you have food and so it doesn't have to start saving fat for another time (as in the caveman times!). Sometimes, not all the time, the morning has been busy with a brisk walk and the demands of a day, so a light snack before lunch keeps me going. Something like nuts or fruit. I eat a lunch, and then the bewitching hour about 4 p.m. hits hard.

I have to *pre*-plan a snack for this time of day. I just have to watch that any snack I have during the day is little and light . Then a lighter dinner than in the past, and a pre-planned "dessert" that is usually a seasonal fruit. (I loved baked apples with cinnamon.)

Notice the word "pre-plan." That has been one of my greatest aids in this process. When I walk into the kitchen, I know exactly what I am going to eat. It has been pre-planned. Nothing else can grab me or distract me from my plan. (At least, that is the hope!) This takes time and intentionality each day and each week. "Saturday or Sunday are usually my preparation days for the week.

My *fourth* observation was that I tended to eat seconds and even thirds when the meal was served on a platter at the table instead of an individual plate. I'd dip in and double dip-in a bite or an extra serving here and there. That's when I changed for the most part to plates with single servings and not putting the serving dish on the table. This added to my awareness. (In fact, sometimes I put cellophane on the dish and put it into the refrigerator before we even sit down to dinner. Then it is not there when I clean up.)

Fifth, I noticed that when I sat down to eat with others, that my servings were always bigger than others. Also, I would always finish everything on my plate. In fact, it was flabbergasting to me how someone could actually leave food, tasty food, on their plates and walk away from it.

Gwen Shambley, who wrote the diet book Out of Egypt, notes that people who can leave food on their plate have what she calls a "thin-mindset." I always had a "need-more mindset." That drives me to want to eat it all!! After all, you can't waste food.

Sixth, I became aware of the size of my meals each day. Breakfast was small, lunch a little bigger and then dinner the largest meal of the day. Research has shown that people who reverse this order have more significant weight control and loss.

There is something they discovered about the digestive properties of the body. They tend to digest food more efficiently (thus less hanging around to produce fat) in the morning compared to the evening.

Perhaps it is because we are more active in the morning, but this research has shown that it is more than this. It has to do with the way our body works differently in the morning than in the evening. I want my body working for me and not against me!

Now I try to eat a substantial, protein-filled breakfast. Then I realize that dinner doesn't have to contain many different items. The vegetables and fruits can be eaten during the day for fuel and lighter eating can take place in the evening.

Seventh, I also noticed that "God made" foods have fewer calories than processed-man-made foods. In fact, I began to calorie count some of the meals that I often consumed.

One meal often gave enough calories for the entire day!

How does anyone stay healthy and sleek eating out and consuming all those processed foods? It's impossible!

I love the fact that many fast-food restaurants are putting the calorie count on their menus. For example, Costco has put the calories up on their price and menu board. It's really shocking. One piece of their pizza is 760 calories. My favorite, the Chicken Bake, is 770 calories. (I confess, I splurge sometimes, but know that the rest of the day I need to adjust to accommodate that many calories from just one meal. That definitely is my carb treat for the week!)

I'm grateful (sort of) that reality is being shown. With these big numbers to tell the calories, truth is right in from of me. It can't be an unaware area of my life any more. Most people don't even think about calories when they order fast food.

I used to be able to shop without my reading glasses, but now I need them on each isle. I take a look at the calorie count and the salt amount and nutritional values of each food. Not every yogurt is created equal.   Not every organic chicken sausage is created with health in mind.   I have finally discovered some foods that are on the "more-healthy" side and provide the protein and lower salt I am pleased to use to fuel my body.

My *eighth* realization is still a problem for me today. I eat too FAST. This may stem back to my days as a waitress where we had to eat between customer needs. (I worked my way through college working at Knotts Berry Farm Chicken Dinner Restaurant and then at a local fish restaurant.)

I am still working on putting my fork down between bites and taking smaller bites. When I say WORKING ON.– this one needs a lot of work, just ask my family.

These observations really helped me to see where I needed to start on my new eating plan. In no way have I become perfect, but I have some specific goals to work towards. I just try to be aware, to consider what fuel I am putting into my body and especially HOW MUCH because I REALLY DO EAT THAT MUCH!!

Myth # 4

Food Gives Me Something I Need

Years ago, I learned the term "co-dependent" – and that I was one!   I was told that I allowed certain behaviors from those around me because I "got something" from them.   I received a certain form of satisfaction or self- worth from helping others with their issues. If those issues were gone, I would lose my purpose or place in their life.   Being co-dependant was definitely an unhealthy way to live.

After working through many issues in my relationships (with many more to come, I'm sure), this same idea reared its ugly head into my relationship with food.

I must be *getting something* besides fuel, as unhealthy as that seems, from the food I was choosing to consume. It's been said that creamy, soft foods like soup or my favorite, chicken Alfredo, offer a feeling of being nurtured. Then the crunchy foods like popcorn and peanuts offer some relief to those feeling aggression.

In the play, *Sound of Music*, Maria sings a song of delight about being married to Captain von Trapp. She sings, "*Nothing comes from nothing, nothing ever did, so somewhere in my youth or childhood, I must have done something good.*"

Nothing comes from nothing. Nothing ever did. So what we are "getting" is coming from something – but what is that something? Attached to various foods are the emotional ideas that we are "getting something" that we are missing, that we want, that we have convinced ourselves we need. (The limbic system once again plays a big part in this.)

Steve Artreburn, from New Life Ministries, offers a conference called, "Lose It For Life." He talks about his own struggles and then his victory with his weight issues. (He also talks about this on his 20-year old call-in radio show that offers life changing counsel with outstanding Christian counselors. www.newlife.com)

In this week-long conference (or video series you can purchase), he makes a statement that hit me hard.

He said, most people eat to get the nutrition they need. However, overweight people need to get something from their food.

Food is not just to meet my hunger needs or even my nutritional needs. I NEED to GET SOMETHING - comfort, pleasure, revenge, whatever, from it. We ask food to give us something that it can't give.

Maybe for a few moments, we get pleasure from the taste and the thrill of stealing a bite of something that has been forbidden, but:

"A moment on the lips is forever on the hips." as the saying goes.

Also, as the old expression goes, "You can't get blood from a turnip." That is exactly what we are trying to do – get something from food that it can't possibly give us.

My friend told me a story about her eating issues. She said her grandmother and she used to fix all kinds of fun recipes in her kitchen. Those were very fond memories for her. Now her grandmother is gone, and she misses her terribly.

When she goes into the kitchen and decides to make those famous "Grandma oatmeal cookies' or "apple pie like only grandma can make," she is "getting something" from that experience. The memories, the fondness of those times, all come back to her and she embraces the love she has for her grandmother each time she makes and eats those memory recipes.

I "get from" food as well. I know my hubby loves oatmeal raisin cookies. We don't need to eat them, but sometimes I will just want to give something to him and then he just seems happier. (Remnants of co-dependency!)

I am hoping to get something from him , and that's not love, it's co-dependency. So the oven is turned on, the oatmeal is taken out, the ingredients are mixed. Soon the cookies are being devoured! The whole time, I think these cookies will meet a need.

When I EXPECT my food to do something for me, food then has power over me.

I often wonder how thin people resist. How do they leave food on their plate? How do they say NO to desserts? How do they limit their portions? Well, I realized, (and here it is, drum roll, please) they are not trying to *GET SOMETHING* from their food.

These people are just satisfied with the source of fuel and energy that food gives them. However, truth be told, I want MORE from my food. What I am trying to GET is beyond nutrition or feeling satisfied. It is an emotional "getting!" I think the food will give me something I am feeling I need. However, in the long run, the food won't and can't give me what I think I need. At first, it will feel good – but soon it will wear off.

Learning the skill of "getting" my needs met in an appropriate way was a hard lesson to learn. It starts with awareness of this as a problem. What am I trying to get from the food? What is it that I really need?

Seeing food differently is a part of this journey. Food does give us something -- fuel – but not the other things we are expecting to get from it. A transformation can take place in me from my aggressive need to "get something" from the food to simply having a gentle appreciation of the food itself.

I don't "stop to smell the roses" when it comes to food. Feeling the fuzz on a peach, biting into the crispness of an apple, mushing the texture of a banana between your teeth, grating carrots over your salad, and carving pieces of a juicy steak – all can add to the experience of eating where you don't need to "get something" from your food.

Enjoy, yes, but don't expect from the food what it can't give. Fuel is its purpose.

For me, this required slowing down. Appreciating the food during the cooking process and then eating it more slowly with time to savor the taste, smell and color. This has led to a great transformation of my thinking and thus my eating patterns.

I have been learning to put my fork down
between bites, commenting to my husband
or others about the flavor, and finding
a new appreciation for the purposes of food.

A realization needs to take place in me – to see what can actually help meet my reality needs and not making food into a fantasy need-meeter.

When this happens, I will begin to believe,
I don't really need this.
In fact, it won't meet what I really
need at this moment.
I don't want to be fooled.

Myth # 5

Feeling Hungry Means I Need To Eat!

The other day I had a nice breakfast. Good proteins: eggs, organic chicken sausage, peppers, and tea. Filling meal? YES! Should I have been content? YES! But I wasn't.

Over the years, I have noticed that I often feel like a bottomless pit that just can't be full. You probably won't hear me say, "I'm stuffed!" (Maybe only after a binge to end all binges!)

I have had to learn to define the feelings I am experiencing in my gut. Some of those feelings say, *YES, it is time to fuel up. I need to eat something.* However, most of the time I really don't need to eat. Something else needs to happen. Defining what the *something else* is can be key.

It took me a while to identify these "something-else" feelings, so I used to just go eat each time I felt the urge to eat. (*Yippee,* I thought. *I'm hungry so it's okay to eat.*) Hold on here and get-a-grip!

Actually, the first "false sign" I had to learn to identity in my gut as not really being hunger was kind of embarrassing and fooled me so many times. It was really a need to have a bowel movement. (Sorry for the gross realities of life!) I would feel hungry – and it wasn't really a realistic time to be hungry – like after a nice-sized meal.

There is no way I should have been hungry. I was feeling something going on in my stomach. Right! The movement of my bowels to be emptied. Think about it. How long after you feed your dog do you need to let him out to do his business? We might have a similar pattern.

Many times, instead of reasoning these gut feelings out appropriately – that I really *couldn't* possibly be hungry – I decided to eat something. Then I felt foolish realizing that -well, it was just time to go! I felt regret over being "foiled" once again by the false gut feelings.

Right after you eat, you don't feel full. It takes a while for the food to arrive in your stomach, the place you "feel" your need for fuel. Lately I have started telling myself, *It's on its way. No need to eat more.*

Being tired also comes across to me as hunger.

My body is trying to tell me something and over the years I have begun to interpret weariness as, *I'm hungry. I just need to eat something.* I don't like to take naps. It makes me feel so groggy the rest of the day, so I keep telling myself that I am not really tired. I have learned I have to at least slow down and read a chapter in a book or even try to take a short nap instead of rushing to the kitchen.

Sometimes that tired feeling is just a tiredness of routine. Writing as much as I do each day, being on the computer, and then grading papers equates to a lot of sitting. That routine can make anyone feel lethargic. Lethargy can take me to the kitchen as well. In that case, I don't need fuel as much as I need movement!

Actually my body is telling me a break is needed. Not a

break to eat, but a break to walk or clean or collect the trash. Something to get moving! When I stopped to realize the real reason for the "hunger" and made the decision to move, this hunger thought soon passed. Distractions work wonders!!

I just got a call from a friend who said she has implemented my "basket of distractions" idea. I put quick ideas to do (instead of eat) on 3 X 5 cards and keep them in a basket by the kitchen door. She said it has saved her six times this week. These distractions have saved me many times as well.

Another feeling that caused me to think I was hungry involved a pull on my emotions. My past has been so full of unfulfilled relationships and times of hurtful and negative relationships. Food became my friend, as I have shared, so whenever I felt hurt or left out, it was natural for me to feel hungry for relationship. Instead of going to a person, I would go to food which had become my new friend.

In fact, I think that is how my whole food issue began. Empty and hurtful relationships were soon replaced with food as a pseudo- relationship. Food can't hurt us like people wound us. Actually, quite the opposite was true. Food is the counterfeit.

Feelings of disappointment, anger, loneliness, and rejection lead me to feel very "hungry." Yes, I was hungry, but it was emotional hunger -- not a feeling that food could ever fill. In fact, with food, more and more is always needed as with drugs. I could never be satiated.

That type of hunger is never satisfied. However, identifying the feeling for what it really was moved me towards a working-it-out instead of a going-around and not through the concern.

Take the time to ask yourself the key question:

What am I really feeling?

You might even put that question on your refrigerator. In counseling I learned that I was so hungry for positive relationships that I never wanted to feel hungry. Hungry feelings triggered sadness from past abandoning relationships. Eating made me feel full, but I was still relationally empty. I love learning truth about myself. It's so freeing.

Here are some of my answers to that question:

I am feeling a heavy stomach. A bowel movement will probably be soon. I should have a hot cup of tea to help promote that digestive move instead of eating something that will just increase that heavy feeling.

OR *Okay, I realize that my husband just said something hurtful to me (unknowingly). I don't need to eat. I need to go and share with him how I am feeling. That relationship needs repair.* (That's taking a risk, so eating is a lot easier.)

OR *I have been so busy this morning, I haven't taken a people break in a long time. I need to call someone or get out and walk with a friend.*

OR *I have been sitting for two hours. I need to get up and move.*

OR *I haven't gotten enough sleep this week. I need to rest my body. It is crying out for rest, not food.*

It is a myth that each time you feel hungry you should eat something. I had to train myself that it was okay to feel hunger - not to feel famished - but hunger, long enough to identify the real cause of that hunger.

Getting my attention away from thinking food will solve the undefined and frustrating feelings I am having is key to moving towards health and weight loss.

Myth # 6

I don't see any harm in being overweight! It's not so bad!

After years and years of failure in the dieting-and-losing-weight-and-gaining-it-back world, I just felt like I wanted to give up. It was hopeless. Dieting caused me to gain more weight than before! Lose it, gain it back, lose five, gain eight, lose and gain more and more. I would see the scale fall down and then creep back up again. Is there any doubt why I wanted to give up on this cause as hopeless?

My solution? I just resigned myself to always be fat. Why fight it?

If God wanted me thin, He would give me what it takes -- self-discipline and a hate for anything with sugar in it. Right?

Since that didn't seem to be happening, I did a great job of rationalizing my always-fat- fate. Nothing mattered anymore. All hope was gone. After all, I had success in my life in other areas; this one I would just have to let go.

As a result of this thinking, no food became off limits to me. Nothing held me back. I would just be who I was obviously created to me – the larger woman, the one who would always carry the extra weight, the one who shopped in the larger-sized section.

I reasoned to myself that maybe if I just didn't think about it so much, just gave in and didn't tie up so much emotional and thought-energy into this battle, I would be freer to do the things of God. After all, human nature tends to move towards what is forbidden.

With this said, after a few weeks, here was the scoreboard: SAD- 100. Christie - 0.

SAD, the "Standard American Diet, was winning. It includes the food in the center of a grocery store: processed, full of the forbidden ingredients –including so much added sugar that taste so good and puts on the pounds. I was ready to give in. If you can't beat them, then join them, right?

What difference does it make anyway? Is all this fight for being fit worth it? If the battle is hopeless, why go to war? Just surrender. If it was hopeless, why should I order a salad when we eat out, when I could order a juicy hamburger.

The days of eating fruit when everyone else had salty, crunchy chips were over in my mind.

It was with that attitude that I set off to find some freedom from the restrictions I had put upon myself for so many years. After all, I had given it many good years of trying. Resigning myself to defeat was – big SIGH – a much relieved place to be. Freedom at last!

Or so I thought! Let's just say that this is a good place to ask once again Dr. Phil's favorite question: "How is that working for you?"

After a few weeks of trying this hopeless thinking, I had to admit – *THIS ISN'T WORKING....AT ALL!* I'm eating like I am making up for lost time. Every forbidden food is occupying my time, mind, plate, and shopping cart. I was quickly out of control.

Even after only a few weeks of the SAD diet, I could sense something vitally wrong. Where I thought I was inviting a new freedom into my life, there was actually no freedom. In fact, there was also no peace and no real joy as I thought there would be.

Worse than that, and by far the most dramatic consequence of this abandonment to reasonableness, I saw my soul slipping away. Satan loves the SAD system. It takes away brain power, health, vitality. AND it deadens the soul.

Scripture puts it this way: It brings "leanness to our souls" – also called a wasting disease.
(Psalms 106:15)

It reminded me of Moses's time in Exodus 16 when the people begged for meat. The manna from heaven was no longer satisfying to them. They were discontent and begging for meat, meat, and more meat! They were tired of the heavenly manna God had been providing for their health and wellness.

They began to pout, cry out, and complain. "This manna stuff is just not making it for us!" (Paraphrase) God heard their complaints. He granted their wishes. He gave them meat until it came out of their nostrils!

While God eventually gave them meat, the Psalmist clarifies the consequences of their discontent with manna. *"But they craved intensely in the wilderness and tempted God in the desert. So He gave them their request, but He sent a wasting disease among them (leanness to their souls)"* I resonated with this idea of "leanness in my soul" as this is the same thing happened to me. It is the saddest place to be after really knowing the fullness of the Lord in my soul so many ways.

Having leanness in your soul is not a pretty place to be —especially when you value your relationship with the Lord and His goodness in your life –especially when you have had a richness from the Lord in your soul that was precious, and you see it slip away.

This leanness is subtle. It comes on slowly. It doesn't seem to be happening until one day you wake up feeling raw, empty, alone, and reaping the consequences of your choices. That's what happened to me.

I felt like David pleading with God, *"Do not cast me from your presence. Please don't take away your Holy Spirit from me"* (Psalm 51:11). You feel very far from God's presence. A gap subtly enters. You feel like you are losing your grip.

I could have seen this coming. Paul spells it out very clearly! If you walk in the flesh, you will have the results of the flesh. (Romans 8:13) That's a promise.

God basically told the Israelites, *Okay, you can have what you want – go for it – but realize that this choice will bring a leanness to your soul.* Your mind, your emotions, your inner being, your will, your very SELF will be torn asunder. Life will become base. Lean. Not rich and full as God would love to give us.

Peter warned about this focus on the flesh as well in I Peter 2:11. "...Keep clear of the desires of your lower nature (sinful passions), for they are always waring against your soul."

What does it mean to have leanness in your soul? I can just speak from my own experience coming to this place of discontent. I felt empty. The fullness of joy in knowing the Lord was dwindling away. His presence was fading – being covered over with "other" things.

The Word was no longer my delight. His Holy Spirit was no longer teaching me wonderful things from His scriptures. I didn't hear the prompting of the Holy Spirit speaking into my heart and mind with His gentle words. My independent spirit started to sound like a "noisy gong or a clanging cymbal." (I Corinthians 13) Feeling love was a stretch. Peace was diminished.

Essentially, I felt like I was floating to nowhere. There was no strong foundation or place to stand firmly. Insecurity reigned! My hopeless stance brought me the exact opposite of what I hoped would happen.

> ### *Believing the myth that change*
> ### *isn't possible –is hopeless – and giving up*
> ### *letting all restraint go just to get*
> ### *what you think you want, is not the answer.*

A life of bingeing on food that you thought would taste so great and would meet the empty spots in your heart and soul, reaps only bitter disappointment.

Notice that the Israelites were deeply entrenched in ungrateful complaining in this process of asking for meat. Their focus was not on what they had, but on what they wanted. You don't see one word of gratefulness in their conversations with Moses or God during this time. Discontent and complaining ruled the day. (Exodus 16)

The turn around to this giving up and going after all you want no matter what, is to focus once again on God's provisions: His plans, His ways, His power, His care. To believe with Mary that "all things are possible with God" (Luke 1:37).

I Corinthians 13:13 tells us, *"In this life we have three great lasting qualities: faith, hope and love."* (Phillips translation)

Hopelessness should never find a place in our relationship with an eternal God.

Beginning to thank Him was my first step to turn a heart around. What I had began to seem greater than it ever did before. I had to believe that God *will* make a way. Your defeats of the past are just that – in the past. There is new hope for today. His lovingkindness and compassion never cease and are new each morning. (Lamentations 3:22-23)

When I realized what was happening, how things had changed, I knew exactly what I needed to do. I had to acknowledge this condition of my life and heart. I needed to CONFESS. I was wrong. I let defeat win over my good judgement and my faith.

I needed to believe that GOD CAN AND WILL MAKE A WAY FOR ME – even me with my years of defeated eating practices. With my pounds of extra fat and flab. Even with my strong, independent spirit.

God is the God of fresh starts,
a God of all hope.

Jesus' death on the cross won this grace of new beginnings for us. I put a wall between my Lord and me, and I needed to get back into His presence.

Confession was step one. Step two was beginning to exercise gratefulness again instead of complaining. Step three was asking God what was THE WAY...the how....the direction to go from here. His way. His new HOPE.

My ways were obviously NOT working. My rationalizing, trying to figure it all out, giving in to what was easy – all were sources of defeat and moved me away from God.

The journey back begins with one step towards Him. This

journey may begin again every ten minutes – or even every minute or day – or every week of our life. It means acknowledging our need of Him and turning towards Him for forgiveness and direction. (And then thanking Him for that forgiveness and grace.)

With this realization and turn around, He began to change my heart and gave me new hope. Now I was very open for God to show me HIS WAY.

He will make a way. It is never too late.
There is never anyone of His children
who needs to feel hopeless.
If you hear the myth of hopelessness
in your heart, it is the enemy
trying to bring leanness to your soul.

Myth # 7

People only see my fat!

When you look into a mirror, what do you see? I saw two things. My nose and my fat. In my mind, that became ME. A big nose surrounded by lots of fat. How sad!

I didn't see the kind me, the spiritual me, the maturing me, the caring me, the intelligent me, the serving me, the creative me, the growing me. I saw a nose and fat! I also believed the myth that when others looked at me, they saw the fat and the nose as well.

How destructive this can be! I am not my nose. I am not my fat! It has taken a long time to move into a place of seeing myself differently. Perhaps this journey started when I met Christ as a senior in high school through the ministry of Young Life. It didn't take the leaders long to clearly see the greatest need in my life was to believe that I was "fearfully and wonderfully made." (Ps. 139:13-16)

As a senior in high school, my small group explored these verses many times to see what this meant to each one of us. *I am fearfully made.* (My brother used to say... "YEP, she's fearful all right. We fear what she will do next!") He was a real teaser, but that is not at all what "fearfully" means.

FEARFULLY means that I am precious in God's eyes. When

He created me, I was the product of much thought, love, future-hopes, and care. My DNA didn't travel down an assembly line where they threw on this nose or these legs, or those hips, or that hair. Every part of me was PLANNED with great FEAR as to how I would be instrumental and purposeful for the glory of God in my time on this earth.

Just to prove that there are no rejects to this creation process, God went on to say I was WONDERFUL!. He looked at the finished product - ME - after giving much fearful thought to ME - and said - *SHE IS WONDERFULLY MADE!* (*Now if God could get me to really believe that!*)

Who am I to look in the mirror and think: *Oh, I hate my nose! I hate my tendency to gain weight.* God gave me great thought. It is all part of the total ME. (We can ask him about those noses and hips when we get to heaven if that is still valuable to us up there.) Until then, self-acceptance and gratefulness for how God made me needs to be set lose in my life.

Looking again in the mirror, I am convinced that the women in my family have extra muscles in their legs. Sturdy legs, as I have come to fondly call them, is a family trait that the women have in common. My cousin Donna, who I loved and who kept her figure beautifully even after having four babies, also had the "family legs."

I carry much of my extra weight in my legs and that has been something hard to accept. (It really shows up when we are at the beach or in the hot tub!) So when I look into the mirror I see parts of me – nose, legs, hair, and yes, fat! I am sure that is all that others see as well. That is a pretty self-involved focus that really doesn't lead anywhere good. Yesterday, a friend who also struggles with her weight said someone told her to "just get over it." I'd say something more. Get on with healing it.

In those small group times with my amazing Young Life leaders, I started to realize that when people SEE me, they don't see ONE part of me. They see the ENTIRE me.

They see the ME that relates to them in an endearing way. They see the love I have for them. All through my life they see my devotion to God and the dedication I have to them as a mother, wife, friend, teacher, mentor, co-worker.

When I allow myself to move into this place of TOTAL-NESS, I see the world differently. I see myself and my place in my world that surrounds me very differently than just as a nose and fat. I see that I have purpose, meaning, influence, and that I am more than just big legs and wimpy hair in the sphere of influence God has placed before me. That those things are not all people see.

I see a part of doing life with the people I love is to live not as a group of parts I wish I could change, but a total person God uniquely created. Even beautiful and thin women say they want to change at least one thing about themselves.

No one seems happy with the FEARFULLY AND WONDERFULLY person God made them to be.

I do have to admit, though, that I am the one who added the extra layers of fat to this wonderfully-made creation. That is a reality I face every day when I see what I look like in the mirror.

While I tried to lose weight before my wedding over 39 years ago, I didn't quite reach my goal weight. I was sad and felt so heavy. Years later, I asked my husband if he felt I was overweight on our wedding day.

Either I have trained him well, he has no memory, or he was being honest. He said, "You were perfect. I didn't think you were overweight at all." While I was focusing on the unwanted fat, he saw the total person he was marrying. THAT IS THE KEY.

Others see the total person, Christie Miller, and how I relate to them. Before I got a handle on the Total ME, I felt like a chicken cut into pieces! Not any more.

Now I tell my students, "Years from now, when you think back about our relationship together, learning and growing and discovering together through the medium of literature, you won't remember just one feature about me. You will remember the total 'essence' of who I was to you as a total person. You will remember our times together, my responses to you, my encouragements, my ideas and thoughts, my motivations for you, and much more." I will remember my students in the same way.....all 3,500 of them in my 37 years of teaching English.

There is one student's work that I will never forget. After talking about this topic of self-image and self-esteem while studying various characters from literature, the students had to write an essay. When this one gal wrote her essay, she didn't know quite how to spell "self- esteem," so she spelled it "self of steam!" I laughed so hard, and realized that self-esteem can swing the other way and be a "self of steam!" — a bunch of hot air as well. She had opened up a new topic for discussion.

When I look into the mirror, their words
might flash through my mind, and I can
choose to believe them instead
of seeing myself how God sees me.

One time I just stood in front of the mirror asking myself, "What do you see?" Am I seeing more than fat and a nose? Who is this person staring back at me? Am I looking at the entire person? Yes, there are people who only see my fat! Their comments can be quite wounding.

(Now that I look back at the cruel words that have been spoken to me, I realize that they probably don't see themselves as total people either. They probably look into the mirror and see their nose or even their fat.)

Our whole person needs nurturing, so we need to see ourselves as a whole person. When I only saw my FAT, I only tried to nurture that part of me. That's maybe why food has been such a huge part of my life.

When I read the verse, "seek ye first the Kingdom of God," I had to be honest with myself and admit that my focus was on me and my fat. THAT was my "seek first!" motive. My fat had stolen my attention. I went for years only focusing on what I saw in the mirror—fat which was the result of my over-eating!

James does talk about mirrors. He tells us to not forget the sort of person we see in the mirror -- not fat or big-nosed, but the "sort of person." Character was his focus. Who are we, not what we look like! What sort of person am I? One that chooses to focus on food and body instead of vigorously focusing on the Lord and loving others.

When I walk away from the mirror, I need to not forget the "sort of person" I am. This is where I enter into a partnership with God to transform the areas of need in my life — for my character to receive a make-over.

Funny thing, or perhaps a delightful thing, when we focus on the Lord's work in our life, on our character, the food issues seem to take a back seat!

When "fearfully and wonderfully
made" meets "seek ye first"
amazing things can happen in a life.

What do we do first? Seek Him first, then you will embrace that you are not a nose and fat but are fearfully and wonderfully made for more than that!! That's the journey I am taking. Want to join me?

Myth # 8

My past has nothing to do with my weight issues.

Another one of my loves in life is directing drama productions with kids, something I have done for over 21 years. This career in drama all started when one of the parents in our community asked me why every play for kids had a few stars and then lots of mediocre, few-lined parts.   She asked me a challenging question: "Why can't there be a play where all of the kids have great parts?"

I took that challenge on!   I wrote a play called, "The Unlegendary Legends of the West."   (And I have been writing plays with this goal in mind since!)   In this play, we covered 75 years of wild west history with the 25 kids who were involved each playing more than one part.

There were no stars, no prima donnas, and every kid had lots of lines and times on stage.   The production of this play was great fun. – until one performance had a hitch – a panic spot! (We laugh about it now!)

In this one wild west scene, Billy the Kid was getting arrested. The sheriff put handcuffs on him and walked him down the isle and off stage. As he was coming down the isle, I asked my husband, who was filming the production, where he put the keys to the handcuffs. He froze for a moment, put down the camera and said, "I'll be right back." They were on his dresser at home.

This became the challenge. Would he get back with the key in time for this character to go back on stage in his new roll as a local miner? The answer was no, and what unfolded is now hysterical, but wasn't too funny at the time.

Billy the Kid rushed into the dressing area and got help putting on his next costume, because, of course, his hands were handcuffed behind him. His long coat had to go over his shoulders instead of putting his arms into the sleeves. We put on a different hat and to top it off, a mustache. He was now ready to go back on stage transformed from a criminal to a gold-finding miner, still hoping that my husband would make it back in time to unlock the handcuffs.

That didn't happen in time, so onto the stage he went -- hands still stuck behind his back covered by his coat. During the scene, which was going well for a while, his mustache began to loosen. It was flopping here and there as he said his lines with great expression. He had no hands free to fix it. His face was contorting over and around trying to get the mustache back into place.

Finally, the female actress on stage with him leaned over and gently pushed the mustache back on. The audience roared with laughter!

I was so proud of these kids because they gracefully went on with the scene. I thought to myself: *Someday we are going to laugh about this – but not right now!*

Years later, this scene came back to my mind. I was reading Philippians 4 where Paul says, "I leave the past behind with my hands outstretched to what God has for me. (Philippians 4:14)

Since I was having trouble leaving the past behind, this verse resonated with me. I wanted to move on to my present – into my future – and to just forget the past. My past had all sorts of wounds, regrets, and broken areas of my heart, and I thought this verse told me that I should be able to just move on! That was the myth I believed for many years. My past has nothing to do with my future. I just wanted to move on.

Some people kept saying to me that I would
need to go back and receive some healing for the past,
but I really didn't want to take that journey as
there were parts that were really painful.

I just wanted to optimistically move into my future like it seemed this Philippians verse was saying to do.

Then God brought the picture to my mind of the miner with his hands handcuffed behind him and his crocked mustache. He couldn't reach out like Paul suggested - he was still tied up - handcuffed behind his back.   That is exactly how I felt. I didn't sense a real freedom to move on, to reach forward.

There was unfinished work in my heart –
in my past – holding me back like the handcuffs.

It was a painful realization to admit that I couldn't fully embrace the future until the past had been addressed. I can remember thinking, *This is going to take forever. It is going to be so painful going through the wounds of the past. I began to wonder how I could avoid all of this pain.*

However, that wasn't the case at all. God's grace filled this process, and at the same time as He began to heal the past He also began to release me from my drives to eat.

One counselor told me that I was "feeding my mother wounds." What's that all about? I needed to find out if healing was to take place in this area. As my "mother wounds" were healed, a new freedom from food was released.

It is a myth that there is no connection with the past and the choices we make each today. A journey back is necessary for healing. First, though, you need to know that you cannot travel this backward journey alone. I had to surround myself with safe and caring people. I call these people "Jesus with skin on" – people with whom I could process my past.

This could take place in a 12-step group (for Christians), a small group which is committed to the healing process through Christ and where people know and care about you, a Christian counselor, a specific Christian healing retreat for this purpose, or any other groups God opens up for you to attend. Pray and ask God for this group.

He offered this support for me in all of the above ways. I needed every one of them to help me receive the healing I needed. A counselor, the right counselor, for a part of the journey; a 12-step group to get me started focusing on my past; a continuing small group where the members were willing to get to know me (and loved me anyway!); and various other opportunities for growth that God brought into my path at the right time.   I watched for these eagerly to become a part of my life.

Note that in the process of finding this type of group, I found more Christians who were in denial than those who truly wanted to face their pasts. They were the *'don't think too deeply about life"* -- the past, present or future.

I want to give you some freedom here. It is okay to not commit to the first small group you visit. You might try ten groups before you find the one that will be your go-to group that fits where you are in your life right now. What is critical to you is that you are going through this look backwards WITH people who understand the need to travel through the process of healing past wounds.   This is the key.

I had to realize these truths in this healing process:

1. The Lord will give me grace beyond all that I ever imagined. I didn't feel alone on this journey. A sense of acceptance and courage accompanied me as I headed into the dark waters of my past. In fact, His grace allowed me to travel through the pain of exploring my past with great courage. Grace is defined as unmerited favor but also as a power that only God can give you. I often cry out, "Grace, please Lord. I need your grace right now."

2. I tended to brush off the pains of the past because when I looked at them with my adult eyes, they didn't seem important. They seemed almost trivial to bring up. However, in this journey, I needed to try to see the past from my little girl eyes. How did you feel as a child? I gained greater understanding, compassion, and healing when I asked this question. After all, it was my child-self that needed to be healed if that is when the wounding happened. I had to allow myself to see life as a child.

A counselor friend of mine shared that she was having trouble getting a client to see life from his past as a child. This man's father had gotten into the car one day and then just drove away – never saying a word – then no contact for 20 years. The man in the counseling office couldn't seem to allow himself to feel the devastation this must have been to him as a child. He saw it with adult eyes, and he wouldn't let himself be affected by it. However, seeing it as a child was a different story.

The counselor looked out the window and saw a little boy playing in the park. He was about the same age as the man was when this man's father left the family. She instructed him to go down and watch the little boy playing in the sand box. She then had him picture the father driving away, leaving *this* little boy.

The man broke into tears. He now saw from the eyes of a child and eventually his own child-self how this wound was so impactful in his life. His personal value and worth was dictated by seeing the back of a car! However, with the Lord, no longer will he have to just buck up and move on. He could stop and grieve this pain by feeling it through the eyes and heart of his child-self. It was even okay, in fact important, that he felt the anger of this situation for the fullest healing. Both grief and anger are needed for total healing to take place when there has been a devastating wound.

3. I had to realize that when I bury the wounds of the past without going through a healing, I have buried them ALIVE. They are still in my heart, influencing my choices (such as my eating behaviors) and my reactions to life (such as choosing food instead of facing the truth of how I feel).

When I binge, there is something in me from my past driving me that has just been triggered and invited into my present. (Remember talking about the limbic system?) I tried to bury it, to move on from it, but it is jumping right into my current life circumstances. Usually this happens without my even knowing. It is the acknowledgment of the need to heal that brings it to the surface.

4. I was pleased to find out that the length of pain in my past was much longer than the time it took to heal. In fact, the healing process seemed like a short time of discovery and realization surrounded by grace. One reason I didn't want to go into the past was because it was so painful for so long in my life. Why would I want to go back there? I had to realize that time back then has nothing to do with time in God's healing process. I didn't have to relive my entire middle school years. I just needed to get in touch with the feelings, the pain, and the rejection of those years.

One friend of mine shared that for years she was abused by her grandmother's words and heavy-handed punishments. She was trying to heal in this area and was dreading going back to walk through all of this pain. God was so good. During her healing journey process, she was having a talk/prayer/ conversation with God. This took about seven minutes, and during this short and intimate amount of time, God revealed to her many things about her grandmother that she had never known. As she saw these things, there was a sense of release, love, and forgiveness that rose up in her that was overwhelming and beautiful. She was able to begin to forgive and to release all of her pain in that short time.

It could have come from no other place than from God. Seventeen years of wounds healed in seven minutes. God can and often does exactly this for us when we ask to heal so that we can move on. Other times, He works to heal us in other ways. God will give you His perspective and His forgiving powers to heal. (*The Feelings Discover Chart* can assist you in this.)

5. Forgiveness is a huge part of this healing process. However, I had to realize that I couldn't "muster up" forgiveness and love for someone. It is only THROUGH the cross that I can truly forgive. Just because I felt that I *should* forgive, it didn't mean that I really *did* forgive someone from my past. A willingness to forgive is the first step. However, God had to fill me with HIS forgiveness for this person. It is the power of the cross, not our sense of obligation to obey that releases the forgiveness in our lives. I can't really forgive. The cross working in me can.

I met a precious sister in the Lord at a meeting we were attending a few years ago. It was so sad to hear her story about her son-in-law murdering her daughter. (Could there be anything more devastating to experience?) She emphatically shared how she had forgiven her son-in-law because "she had to obey God."

She said those words, yet I didn't sense the freedom in her words or her demeanor. This crime still held her hostage, but she couldn't acknowledge this. (And I don't blame her for one minute. This was a horrific crime.) The pain, the injustice, the brutality of it all was still bound up in her heart. Forgiveness is a process, a journey you travel through the cross of Christ, not a set of keenly staged words that changes your heart to be able to forgive. It is not an act of just your will, but a change of heart. Forgiveness is a process that takes time.

6. As I often say, God created tears and grief as the key to the healing process. Christian psychologist John Townsend notes in his video series from the book How We Grow that "grief is the pain to heal all other pains." It was designed to wash over the wounds and tenderly soothe and heal them. For years, I couldn't allow myself to cry or grieve. I thought that if I let go, I would never stop crying.

I actually had to learn how to grieve. Today I call it my most important skill to handling life on this planet. Grieve what was. Grieve what isn't. Grieve what is. It should be one of our first lines of defense and healing. (Again, using the *Feelings Discovery Chart* is helpful in this.) Included in that grief is the right sort of righteous anger. Both sadness and anger needed to be embraced as I grieved the past. That was hard for me.

7. I discovered that in this healing process there can't be any blame put on others. The purpose was to see the pain from God's heart and to have Him heal and release *me* from that painful wound. It happened. It can't be reversed. However, it can be healed by God. We might get stuck on blame, but that will only hold up the healing process. Your parents, your friends, your siblings, your classmates, your spouse were who they were, and they did what they did. The issue is not blame, but it is the amazing healing that God offers with His power. He knows the situation and the pain.

If you feel like I felt ---that your hands are tied behind your back – allow God to find the key to releasing them so that you can reach out to the wonderful things He has for you. It requires a searching, surrendering, healing and transforming heart for the process to begin.

A metamorphosis has to take place,
and God is just waiting to do this for you.

Paul did go through this process before he claimed to be able to hold his hands out to whatever God had for him. Going through that process is the first step to reaching "our high calling."

Myth # 9

I'm the only one affected by my being overweight.

Since I consider myself to have an eating addiction, I've read lots of books about combating addictions. In one of these books, the author asked the question: *Have you ever considered the pain you are causing others by continuing in your addiction?*

That question caused me to pause. Really, I couldn't think of anyone I was truly hurting by my being overweight. It's my problem. My burden to carry. *It's not like being a mean alcoholic or a dangerous druggie,* I rationalized.

Then on further thought, I began to get a little more honest with myself. I am hurting someone. That someone is me! I can honestly say that at times when my eating is out of control, I feel like two people. One is my very disciplined, spiritually mature, loving, caring, and a wise woman of God. The other woman is a food addict who often denies her problem. The reality is, the "addicted fleshy woman" does hurt the "other spiritual woman" - ME.

I am hurting who I can become in Christ. I am hurting my relationship to God. My husband might accept me as I am, but my Lord is sad by my fresh-driven choices. He knows I could be so much more than I am. When I take these fleshy detours in life (which I'm delighted to say are now fewer and farther between),

I never know what I will be missing in my life as a result of the choice to binge and escape.

(Just a note: Not all husbands overlook the extra weight. In fact, one friend told me that when she lost quite a bit of weight her husband said it was the greatest gift she could have given him. However, I learned we can't lose weight for someone else. We have to be motivated for ourselves and for the Lord.)

My life verse is I Corinthians. 2:9:
"Things which eye has not seen and ear has not heard, and which have not entered the heart of man, all that God has prepared for those who love Him."

Those things that God wants to do in my life that are beyond my wildest imagination, might be put on hold because I put the flesh first. I'm forgiven, I'm loved, I'm always His child, but I may miss out on the closeness I really do desire deep in my heart as well as some ministry opportunities.

Most of you know that there were two sons in the Luke 15 "Prodigal Son" story. It's very interesting to note that there are two different words for SON used in this passage. The word SON used for the older brother who has been with the father and faithful to him all of this time is a tender, close, intimate word for son. It is like the relationship the Father has for His Son Jesus.

The prodigal is also a son, yet the Greek word is different. It implies some distancing. Yes, he is loved, yes, he is forgiven, and yes he is the father's dear son, but it isn't quite the intimate son that the older brother was to the father. I wonder if my choice to escape into food pulls me away from that intimate position with my Father? This should motivate me to stay on course. To not get carried away with my fleshly eating binges. Believing the myth that I am not hurting anyone and ignoring that it really does hurt me, doesn't help me get motivated to change. In fact, another question I was asked was: "What is motivating you to keep moving towards change and not relapsing into your old patterns? "

When I saw this question, I decided to make a list of motivators that *should* be keeping me on track. I was appalled that none of them really gripped me tightly.....as tightly as I wished they would.

>I want a closer walk with God and choosing flesh over Spirit defeats this goal.

>I want to be healthy, so I can ride bikes and snowshoe for many more years.

> I want to have clarity of mind, not fuzziness. (Too many carbs makes me fuzzy.)

> Each good choice leads to another good choice. Every choice matters.

> I want to glorify God with my life and my temple.

>I don't want others to judge me by my appearance.

>I want to show the power of God in my life by my being healed in this area. In other words, if God can heal me, He can heal anyone!!! His power is that great!!

Evidently, though, while each of these reasons is powerful and very personal, they aren't the thing that keeps me on track. Only God can put into my heart the priority to eat healthy.

Sometimes, Satan feeds me the line that it all really doesn't matter. *It doesn't hurt anyone. It doesn't really make a profound difference in any way. One cookie (or a dozen) or one bowl of ice cream (or three) really don't mean a thing in the vast array of life.* Those are the thoughts Satan, the liar, puts into my mind.

When I listen to Satan's suggestions and lies, I fail. When I believe "it doesn't matter," I lose all motivation to succeed. Only God can put on my heart the drive, the motivation, the determination to seek His help to succeed. Only God. It does matter! I am not the only one affected.

I have been praying first that He would do just that in my life - to keep my motivation going. Then I have been praying that He would help me not believe Satan's lies and to not move into denial that my addiction is not hurting anyone else.

I am a someone and my choices are hurting me. My daughters are watching. God wants to come along side me in this. He wants to keep me living in reality and to keep me strong and motivated.

I want to be that daughter of intimacy. Each choice does count!!

"It is God who is at work IN ME
to will and to do for His good pleasure."
(Philippians 2:13)

Myth # 10

I don't need to tell anyone about this problem of mine.

Secrets! We all have them. I've tried to keep my overeating a secret without much luck. You see, I realized as I am walking around with more weight on my body than is healthy, that this secret of overeating is not really a secret.

You can keep lots of things secret from others, but this one....it is out there for the world to see no matter what clothes you wear to try to cover it up.

For a long time, I felt that my secrets were no one's business. I didn't have to or want to tell anyone that I had a food addiction. That every day I struggled with making good choices and often made some bad ones. When life gave me lemons, I didn't make lemonade, I hit the kitchen for carbs and sugar to numb everything.

I couldn't see any possible reason to bear my soul to anyone but God – no real need to confess to my friends, family, or small group --even to a doctor or counselor. I didn't want to draw attention to the problem.

Probably deep inside, I knew if I told someone then I would have to do something about it. That every day when my friends came to small group or I saw them at events, they would want to ask, "SO.....how are you doing with YOUR problem?"

I didn't want to start this judgment cycle in motion. I had enough self-condemnation than to invite it from others.

Keeping how bad my problem was as a secret was the best route, or so I thought.

That was until I read James 5:16 (Phillips translation): "*You should get into the habit of admitting your sins to each other and praying for each other, so that if sickness comes to you, you may be healed.*"

What did that verse just say? Admit to others that while I have some areas of great success in walking with the Lord, this is my failure area? Their entire image of me will change. I can't do that. I want to keep what semblance of respect and dignity I have. Admitting to being totally out of control with a food addiction – that would just be too vulnerable. Only God will hear this about me. That was enough.

However, that verse had a promise with it. If you confess, you will be healed. Well, I wanted to be healed. I needed to decide if I was going to believe this verse or just ignore it. I choose to believe it.

Also, I realized if I told others, I would receive more prayer if others knew about my struggle. If I kept this secret, I would be the only one praying about this problem for me. I knew that I needed prayer warriors on my team.

What a bold step this would be for me. I had believed the myth for so long that confessing to God was enough. While I'd been vulnerable in other areas to my friends, this one was going to be huge to divulge. Then, again, I had to face it that my problem is already visible to everyone around me, but I guess I lived in denial about that. My creative wardrobe ideas were probably not really covering up that I had a problem in this area. In the past, I had shared some very personal and difficult things with my small group and other friends. I was pleasantly surprised. They had NOT been judgmental. They had loved me in spite of these things. What a great feeling. I asked myself why this would be any different. (At other groups in the past, I had not received this safety, grace and love.)

I decided to do it –to be honest about this secret area of my life. To confess to my friends just how out of hand this problem had become.

My voice quivered as I started to share, but I have to admit, once I started sharing I felt a new boldness. The Lord was encouraging this honesty.

They were awesome. They loved me. They expressed no condemnation. Compassion flowed and then they even came up with some ideas to help me.   They noted that they were only a phone call away. They also mentioned that I loved to write.

Why didn't I journal my experience. Why didn't' I find a new place to GO instead of to the kitchen.   They were on my team. They wanted to help. Their suggestions made great sense.

Perhaps this book is a result of their encouragement to journal.

Now I want to tell you the best part. The James verse was RIGHT. My real healing did not begin until I confessed to these safe friends. Why had I waited so long?

Why had I insisted for so many years only confessing to the Lord? Why had I carried this problem on my own for so long?

The verse says, "confess, admit your sin areas, that you may be healed."   It's clear that real healing won't happen until you make your secret known through confession to others.   I found this to be very true!!   A new power was released through confession.

> *This scripture was not only exhorting me to*
> *confess to others, it was making a promise*
> *to me that this*
> *was the route to healing.*

If I confessed, healing would begin, and that it did!   As I look back, that was the day that real victories and movement toward healing truly began.   While my friends care about my growth in this area, they know that I am *not* my problem. That's not who I am. I am not the fat I carried.

They didn't and don't make a huge deal about it.   There is prayer, there is encouragement, there is come-along-side-me, but it is not all-consuming in our relationship as I feared.

NOTE: If you don't have friends like this who are safe, loving and accepting without condemnation, you need to be cautious. Have the Lord help you build such friendships and even a dynamic small group like this.   Take the initiative and go out looking for such friends and a group. They do exist.

Jesus doesn't condemn (Romans 8:1) so your friends shouldn't either! Pray and seek this type of people to be in your life. The Lord will answer this prayer. Confessing to God was one thing. Telling others was taking it to a whole new level.

I have heard many times and often say in jest, "Confession is good for the soul." Little did I know what a powerful statement of truth that really is. That this idea is scriptural!

It lifts us out of the ruts of our lives, and I can testify that this risk was well worth it.

Change begins with small steps....
although I would consider this a big step.
Taking a risk pulls us ahead –
it changes the picture of the way things are.
Keeping secrets is an enemy to healing.

Myth # 11

More determination is all I need to conquer these habits.

This last spring , we were camping on the sunny side of our state. It had been a pretty wet winter on our side of the mountains, so this sun was a very welcome experience. While relaxing at our camp site in the warmth of the sun, we were enthralled with the birds singing and flitting from tree to tree as if they didn't have a care in the world. Spring had arrived for them after surviving a rough winter.

On the last day of our trip, however, the weather reversed itself. Strong winds, rain, and even snow over the mountain pass came our way to end our trip. Again, I was fascinated by the birds. No longer were they "flitting" from tree to tree and chirping out joyously. They were now in survival mode. The winds were strong. The rain was beating against them.

Their life rhythm had changed. Now they were up against forces over which they had no control. Survival was their new mantra with a great "fight" required to survive.

Then I reflected. This picture is very much like our lives and our relationship with food. When life is going along smoothly – relationships are positive, responsibilities are manageable, our children are making good choices, finances are in some semblance of order, and we feel a presence of the Lord, we are in what I would call a good rhythm. We are chirping in life just like the birds. We can "flit" with the best of them.

However, when the storms come – the raging winds and the pounding rains, we also have to go into survival mode. We need to learn the rhythm of FIGHT. We need to acknowledge that there is a change in the barometer of life. Different choices need to be made. Protections need to be in place. More energy needs to be expended to survive.

When these changes come (relationships, new financial challenges, work going off kilter, etc.), we have to stand up and put forth greater energy so that the storms of life don't destroy the rhythms of our life. We need to learn new rhythms, rhythms that will work for the spring and summer and rhythms that will work during the dark winters and the wind-struck pressures in our lives.

People often ask me to speak to their group about the "seasons of our lives," and what I share with them surprises them. They wanted something relating to time periods of our lives, like teenager, college student, single life, young married, young parents, raising teens, empty nesting, retirement, etc. The seasons of our lives.

However, scripture doesn't refer to seasons in this way. It refers to seasons like a farmer. A dormant time – winter. A preparing the soil time – spring. A tending to the crops time – summer. And a harvesting time – fall. If I embrace the personal -to-me meaning of each of these seasons, then I will be prepared for the storms of life. Life is not lived in a straight line. It is lived with dips and mountains, valleys and hillsides – seasons.

Those of us with eating addictions
have not yet learned the rhythms of life.

Some of us are fine when we can "flit and chirp" in the safety of the sun, but when it comes to stormy days, we head right for the kitchen. Those who raised or discipled us missed teaching us a chapter in the book of life — the dark times of winter – the storms where we have no control over our circumstances. What are we supposed to do? Maybe we never learned how to handle these times in a healthy way.

We fight in all the wrong ways by isolating and trying to escape to food to numb the new pressures.

Our relationships are stressful, too many responsibilities are coming at us, and we cannot feel the presence of the Lord in our lives. We cry out to Him and feel like our prayers are hitting a brick wall.

What is our recourse for being hit so hard? We eat. Our patterns have taken us to the kitchen for so many years that we don't know any other course of action. Our protections are NOT in place.

We start on a new diet, have a new plan, feel a new surge of success in this area, and we know that this time... yes, this time...with this determination...we can succeed. However, the storms come. We didn't prepare for them.

Determination alone cannot help us successfully survive the storms of life. The sooner we realize this and prepare, the sooner we will be able to travel through any season of life without devastation hitting our successes.

What does it mean to PREPARE? To learn the skills of handling pressures? *First,* it means knowing in our minds that at any time the "weather" of life can change. When we go camping, we always bring our awnings with us. We always have our rain gear in the trailer. A change of clothing is always in our suitcases. We have prepared for the change in weather.

Second, we need to monitor our internal "weather." When we feel stressed, we need to name it. What is that stress? We need to be aware of our responses and reactions to the changing weather -- the circumstances of our lives. We don't just hear or feel something and say, "It will be okay." That is denial.

Instead, we sit down with the Lord and talk it out. (Need I mention the Feelings Discovery Chart again?) We identify the type of storms hitting us. How are external things affecting our internal lives?

Then, *third*, and this is the most important step, we call upon our "go-to people" to walk us through this storm. We need to go to the Lord first and then to our go-to people.

They can help us put up the "awnings of protection" and they can help us identify what we are facing and give us some ideas for how we can face it. These people need to be in place long before the weather man warns us that change is coming.

Someone told me that being in a small group from our church is so important because it is not IF problems come but WHEN.

Determination is within yourself. However, you might not have enough of what it takes within yourself to make it through *this* storm. In fact, your past eating patterns prove that you don't have what it takes. Not last time and not this time and not the next time. This outside help, will begin to place this skill into your own heart

You need more training.
Not more discipline but more discipleship.

Finding "go-to people" is not easy. (Forgive me if I repeat that again and again.) They need to be good listeners, have walked through storms of their own, have a commitment to see you through, and to do it all without condemnation. They are safe people. They know how to dish out truth with grace and grace with truth.

They either have the skills or are willing to help you find the skills or even be willing to discover them with you. When the storm hits, STOP - ASK - GO TO and sct up new response patterns.

Stop to evaluate how you are feeling and
what you are thinking. Ask for help.
Go To resources that can assist you.

Counselors will note that the people who recover from difficult time are those who have a multitude of resources available to them. Ask who can best help me in this time of stress? Go to the people God has put into your life for "such a time as this!" Prayer is important. Time with the Lord is key. However, remember that God often works through His children to meet our needs.

Sometimes you have to acknowledge that your determination was blown away when the storm came – sometimes even when the slightest wind or drop of rain began. As you learn to STOP-ASK - GO TO and implement new response patterns, you will see yourself facing bigger and bigger storms of life and surviving longer through each storm. You will visit the kitchen less often to escape the storm. You will be able to face the storm and walk THROUGH it.

When I hear the weatherman in my part of the world (The Pacific Northwest), say, "Rain, strong winds and occasional hail are expected with thunder and lightening for the next two weeks," I don't shrivel up in dread. I implement the steps to get me through, and don't just depend upon my own our determination.

Stop and acknowledge the problem. Define it. Like in Mark 5 where Jesus asked the man, "What is your name?" The answer was "Legion." He defined the problem. He was up against a legion of problems and forces of evil. He then knew with what He was dealing. When we are surrounded by a "legion" we have to STOP – ASK – GO TO.

STOP - Recognize that the "weather" of your life has changed. We are facing some definite challenges. You need some help! Define the problems (storms) you are facing.

ASK - How are you feeling about all of this? Get out your *Feelings Discovery Chart*. Identify your feelings. This identifies what you are up against internally! Ask who can help you in this time.

GO TO - GO TO your safe people who know you, your lure to food, your maturity level to handle storms, and all without condemnation. Talk, share, and all with honesty. Be willing to be vulnerable. When we admit weakness, the Lord comes along side of us with strength, and most often he uses other people to be our GO TO for internal strength.

It is the greatest myth and lie to believe that you have within you all it takes to overcome these habits and response patterns. All sizes of storms will hit, and you need to be prepared to admit your need for help. This leads right into the next myth.

Myth # 12

I just need more Will-Power!

My walks each day (rain or shine) give me lots of opportunities to talk to the Lord about ideas and concerns. There was a great question that came up in our *Lose It For Life Support Group* at church the other night so that was on my mind during this morning's walk.

One gal was commenting about a list that was given in the videos we were watching called, "Seven behaviors that lead to transformation." She was surprised that SELF-DISCIPLINE was NOT on the list. Interesting --since that is what we all say we need to lose weight – more self-discipline and lots of will-power.

Those of us who are overweight often say things like: "If only I had stronger will-power, more self-discipline...." "I just don't have enough self-discipline. That's my problem." "I could stay on a diet if I had stronger will-power!" Have you heard that before or said it yourself? I surely have!!

> *We all start our New Year's Resolutions*
> *with lots of will-power and commitments*
> *to discipline ourselves.*

However, this idea of will-power and self-discipline was NOT on the list of seven key aspects of seeing change happen in our lives. We were puzzled, and we ended the meeting saying that each of us would pray and study this idea to see if God would answer this question:

"What place do will-power and self-discipline have in the process of losing weight?"

It's funny (or sad) that we all know from experience that will-power doesn't work in the long run. However, we tend to depend upon it, and then keep beating ourselves up when we don't have enough of it.

Most counselors will tell you that will-power alone is a false road that leads to failure. However, we start all of our New Year's Resolutions with a lot of will-power statements which soon fizzle out. How soon? Some studies show that will-power fizzles out after three to four weeks on the average. Pretty short-lived when we have a lot of weight to lose.

In thinking about this question on my walk, God reminded me that I had come a ways on this journey. I had been able to see some success. However, as I am writing this, I am currently feeling a real lack of motivation. A stuckness.

My will-power went on vacation, and I am left falling back into my ruts. My will-power and self-discipline drives are fading quickly. DANGER!! I asked myself what role will-power and self-discipline have in this journey we call dieting.

I decided to do some research in scripture on the word "discipline." I also asked the gals in my weekly small group what they thought about will-power.

One of the gals from my small group emailed me some very wise thoughts in response to this question. She said:

"Isn't self-discipline using the flesh to fight the flesh?" YES, YES! Did you catch that? SELF is flesh....so self-discipline is using something fleshly to defeat something fleshly. It just won't work!

She went on to say: "Isn't it a matter of allowing the Spirit to overcome our flesh?" Yes, yes! Will-power and self-discipline are so limited – they only go so far in pushing us to begin to succeed. While they can get us going and work with the Holy Spirit to jumpstart our goals and desires to get a handle on our weight, we need to realize that they descend down.....quickly.

Only the Holy Spirit can stay strong. Using self-discipline and will-power is not God's way for us.

In my study, I found that the word "discipline" is used 73 times in scripture. (7 times in the New Testament, primarily in Hebrews, and 36 times in the Old Testament.) Each and every time, it refers to God disciplining us or parents disciplining their children. It is NEVER used as an exhortation to discipline ourselves. Interesting!

(Paul does use a word one time that is translated discipline in I Corinthians 9:27. "But I discipline my body and keep it under control lest after preaching to others I myself should be disqualified." The context of that verse is an analogy to a boxing match. That word is also translated: "I pommel my body" - "I buffet my body" - "I strike a blow" - "I subdue my body" – saying that he allows it to be bruised for the cause of Christ. And bruised it was. He suffered more persecution and beatings than any other apostle from what we can see in Scripture. This word refers to "allowing" his body to be "wearied, bruised, and kept under control." NASB)

God is *not* calling us to focus on disciplining ourselves or to beat ourselves up. He is *not* asking us to live life motivated only by a disciplined will-power. He wants His Holy Spirit and His love to be the driving force behind change and transformation in our lives. He disciplines! We don't do it to ourselves.

I remember a counselor friend of mine telling me about a gal who came to his office. She was struggling with her weight and she kept saying, "I know I just need more self-discipline. If my will-power would just stay strong." The counselor reminded her that she was looking in all the wrong places for help. If her internal self-discipline was the answer, she wouldn't still have the problems. If she could have fixed it on her own, it would be fixed already.

God's way is self-control, and in scripture we see that self-control is a fruit of the spirit. (Galatians 5:22)

Self-control can be defined as having nothing OUTSIDE controlling us.

We choose to let the Holy Spirit in us drive us, help us choose, give us power. II Timothy 1:4 says, *"For God has not given us a spirit of fear, but a spirit of power and love and a sound mind."* (J.B. Phillips translation) We begin each day surrendering our will to Him, and then stop many times during the day to refresh that prayer.

That leads me to another question. If self-control is a fruit, how do I get more of that fruit on my "tree"? I remembered a lesson I learned years ago from an incident with my lawn mower.

One time I was mowing the front lawn. (I have only done it once as I avoid this job like a plague!) In that one time, I was talking to the Lord about this old apple tree we have in our front yard. Every year this old gnarly-looking-tree produces amazing fruit – year after year, beautiful fruit. I remember as I mowed under this tree that I asked the Lord, "How can I bear fruit like that in my life?"

He pointed out to me the attributes of this old apple tree. It had stayed put, firmly planted, solidly standing for many years. It abided, as it says in John 15:4: "Abide in me and I in you. As the branch cannot bear fruit on its own. It must be abiding in the vine. Neither can you unless you abide in me." (NASB)   That makes sense.   For a tree to bear fruit it must be planted and stay planted.

Also, I observed that this tree was exposed to the natural nutrients from the ground, the air and the sky (including rain!!). It remained in a place where it could receive all it needed to bear fruit. I saw that I needed to plant myself in nurturing places where I could hear God's truth, rub elbows with God's people who know how to walk with Him, and be open to learn and grow.

From this one-time lawn mowing experience, I saw how God was asking me to ABIDE in Him and to EXPOSE myself to His ways, His truths, His people (who offer grace and energy), and His cleansing "rain storms." When these two things, abiding and exposure are in place, I will produce fruit, and especially the fruit of self-control.

Isolation, though we are drawn to it at times, is not a place to be if you want to bear more fruit.
(There is a difference between isolation and alone-time.)

I had to chuckle as I thought about this because self-control is at the end of the list of "fruit" given in Galatians 5. In the past, God has taken me through a cycle of lessons for me to produce each of the fruits (love, joy, peace, patience, kindness, goodness, faithfulness), but it was self-control that seemed to get the short end of the stick in my life being at the end of the list.

God also reminded me that He doesn't give "fruit baskets!" (When I speak at a retreat, I am often given a fruit basket as a precious gift of love from the group.) Fruit is not a gift. It has to come through laborious growth on the tree. The fruits in your life will also have to go THROUGH the processes of growth. It is never hand-picked for you and presented to you in a basket.

So, self-control would not be a gift from God, not a box to open and now own. It would have to come through the process of walking with and abiding in the Lord. Each day a new choice. Each day a new seed of growth on the tree of self-control. It comes through the process of growth.

I realized in thinking about this that I had never asked God for the fruit of self-control in my life. I had asked for patience (which can be dangerous) and for love (which delights God) and for more faith (something we all need), but I had never asked God to produce in me the fruit of self-control. I had looked for it – hoped for it – seen it in others – wanted it – desired it – realized my need for it – but I had never actually asked for THAT fruit of the Spirit in my life.

I am sure that His Spirit has produced some of this fruit in me, but I needed much more. I stopped right there in the middle of the road while on my walk and asked God for a HUGE CROP of the fruit of self-control.

All this is to say that will-power and self-discipline, while sounding like powerful entities, are really false-hopes for change. The more I depend on them and try to work on having more of them, the more I fail in my efforts to lose weight. They deceive me into thinking that I am making so much progress since they make us feel so empowered --at first.

That kind of "power," however, is short lived and like New Year's Resolutions, they quickly fade out.

I had to learn to watch for and identify when I was resting my dieting hopes on will-power and not on abiding in the power the

Lord had to offer through surrender. I saw it when I left prayer and a consciousness of the Lord out as part of my change process. Getting weaker and not stronger is the key: Weaker in Christ and more dependent. I have lost count how many times I caught myself in the will-power trap. It is a sort of "selfie" and not of the Lord.

I have also found from this that it is just as important to know what doesn't work as well as what does work in my quest to lose weight.

Will-power and self-discipline don't work.
They are flesh after flesh.
The sooner I move towards the
REAL SUSTAINING POWER,
the sooner I will get on with my
progress to healthy eating.

Myth # 13

I can never get enough. I'd better be prepared.

It's 4 a.m., and I just woke up thinking about my "adopted" nephew Tim. At this writing, it's been two days since I heard he was killed in a tragic accident at his work. I am writing this chapter in honor of him. My mind is spinning with memories of this always-happy, smiling, gentle soul.

One of my first memories of him was when I was at the dinner table at their home soon after my "adopted" sister brought Tim and his sister Jill home from San Diego where they had just been airlifted from war-ravaged Vietnam. It was the 1970's baby airlift that successfully saved the lives of so many war-traumatized children.

Timmy and Jill, about three and five years old at the time, were sitting at the table, and I watched as they ate a bite of food and then snuck a bite of food into their clothes. This was their survival method. In Vietnam, they never knew if there was going to be a next meal. They always felt that there was never going to be "enough." They continued in this feeling of wondering if there would be "enough" even though the table and the house were full of food items.

When you are always worried that there is not going to be enough, you are constantly thinking of ways to survive that "hunger." My friend Lois, shared with me that she knows this feeling well.

Her mother died when she was just a young girl, and she was needed as the oldest child to raise the younger children. Her father was a dedicated pastor who never made quite ENOUGH money to assure her that there were would be ENOUGH in the cupboards for the family.

She shared with me that was the reason why bottles of ketchup with a half of a tablespoon left were kept in their refrigerator. They may need it during a time that there might not be ENOUGH to buy a new bottle.

The theme of NOT ENOUGH has made
its home in many of our hearts, and it drives us
to certain actions that are not healthy.

The theme of NOT ENOUGH made its home in the heart of Timmy and Jill and my friend Lois (and many of us). It drove them (and us) to certain actions.

I don't know how this has affected Tim over the years, but Lois recently confessed that she still has lots of almost empty jars in her cupboards.

There won't be enough still resonates in her heart.
The fact is, there is never enough to feed a
heart that has a hole in it.

While Tim and Lois were raised with food shortages, many of us were raised with emotional shortages. Somehow we feel we have to make up the losses. There just wasn't ENOUGH love, grace, or security planted into our hearts, and we are always haunted by that NOT ENOUGH feeling.

We have created ways to compensate.....food has become our "filler." We stuff it in, like Timmy and Jill did, to be there in case there is emptiness that needs to be filled.

For years, I have had this driving need to always
feel full. Whenever I was hungry, it produced in me
a trigger. It had less to do with food and more
to do with the emotional emptiness
I had experienced over the years.

That emptiness had settled in my heart, but I mistook it for my stomach. Eating was a way to numb the feelings of emptiness. I didn't want to feel that "not enough love" feeling, so I numbed myself from feeling anything.

As a result, if I felt those same triggers -- the feelings of being unneeded, unwanted, unappreciated, unimportant – not able to meet the standards expected, left out, rejected, marginalized, condemned, and inferior – I interpreted all of these as *I'M NOT ENOUGH*.

I needed to fill myself because
I was not full somewhere in my heart.

I never stopped to ask any questions -- I just went into action. – into the kitchen!

When I felt this way, I didn't stop to think about the cause. I just felt - in fact, intensely felt that I was NOT ENOUGH. Perhaps, somewhere in the past, I cried out for help and my cries were left unanswered. I had to create ways of meeting my own "NOT ENOUGHS."

Keeping filled with food - eating large portions - repeating the lie to myself, *I am just a person who requires a lot of food to keep going in my active life*, was my mantra. I believed that NOT ENOUGH lie for years. It still rises up into my soul to try to haunt me right back into the kitchen.

There, facing the cupboards of temptation, I could fill myself with food... but it would never be ENOUGH to soothe the empty, NOT ENOUGH feelings I had at that moment. I never stopped to identify the feelings. They overwhelmed and I rushed to numb them.

When the binge was over, I would be very full, but still feel empty. Learning the skills, yes, the skills, of *feeding* those empty spots in my broken self was a turning point.

I learned that having an intelligent conversation with myself and the Lord (if I stopped long enough to realize what was emotionally happening), gave me some rational thought to my possible irrational (limbic) about-to-happen behavior.

I just jumped to food to fill me up, never asking what was really empty.

That conversation with the Lord would show me the cause. To go down deep and to find out what it was that just happened to trigger these NOT ENOUGH feelings in my heart. Had someone said something critical to me? Had someone failed to include me? Was I feeling alone? Had I not measured up somehow? What was the level of condemnation versus grace in my life at that moment? What was causing these empty feelings?

When Eve was in the garden, she was not on the look-out for the possible serpents in her life. She was deceived into thinking that *eating* was going to bring her something she thought she needed.

Just think, the garden was a perfect place – perfect –

however, freedom of choice existed. We still have that freedom of choice today. God considers this a good thing, but it has gotten me into lots of trouble. Having a free will can be both good and bad.

Eve was searching for more than God had provided. She was in a NOT ENOUGH frame of mind.

I believe that "not-enough" drive has been haunting women since the Garden of Eden. There are more repercussions from the fall than we usually acknowledge. Now, living in a broken world with more "serpents" than we sometimes feel we can handle, we have to be even more diligent to their deceptions. My serpents come in many forms. Not having ENOUGH is one of my repeated temptation patterns.

I have to admit that the things people say, an attitude, even the look of their eye can trigger my feelings of being empty. This happens less and less now that I have a strong support group of people in my life who stand by me. I don't have to REACT to the "serpents" because I have the pure love of others to counter-balance those attacks. They don't set me off balance as much any more – and being off balance takes me right to the kitchen.

The other "serpent" that triggers me is my inadequacy. When I just don't get things done up to standard (usually someone else's impossible standard) – when I make a mistake (which happens often) – when I forget something (yes, more and more especially since I am getting older) – when I do something that bugs someone (which seems to be often – my personality seems to always get me into trouble!) – voices in reality or in my mind let me know that I was NOT ENOUGH and I feel totally empty.

I may just have accomplished something exciting - a huge

project that will benefit many others - but a totally empty feeling settles in. One part of the project just wasn't right. While it turned out great, in my mind I was NOT ENOUGH – it was NOT ENOUGH.

I feel this need to fill that emptiness. To do this I have choices. I can fill it with so much food that my stomach feels full but my soul still feels like it has not had enough, or I can fill it with truth and reality. I can walk THROUGH it.

That would include accepting the reality that those standards in my mind are too harsh, that mistakes are normal realities in life, that forgetting happens when you are spinning a lot of plates at once and can't afford a personal secretary, and that we live in a broken world where broken people irk each other quite often and that irking is often not as much about you but more about them. That is the rational conversation I need to have with myself and the Lord.

When we have that reality conversation, the Holy Spirit fills us with His compassion and promises to provide comfort for us in this broken world. ENOUGH – just what we need.

This Holy Spirit's filling with compassion is, however, spiritual and not material. It took some time for God to teach me the difference. That my healthy "enough" is not coming from something material, but something that was going to happen inside my soul. God was going to use His comfort and the comfort of others in my life to fill me with "enough" to not need so much food to fill me up.

You can see how this has to be learned. Especially when your habits are set in stone to fill your empty spots on your own by a trip to the kitchen. This new *filling* would have me be full of God which is a new sensation in this area. Instead of food, He feeds me with loving doses using other loving people as tools as well.

For Timmy, it was the belief that his new family was going to provide ENOUGH – everything he needed. In fact, they did, and he grew up to be a wonderful adult. It took a while for him to trust that they would provide, that their provisions would be ENOUGH, but the exchange of this thinking from non-trust to trust took place over time, just as it is happening in me.

I wish that I could explain what being "full" of God is with better words or a clearer picture, but that's hard because it is not material in nature. I can say that it is a satisfaction that food never gave. Food never satiated my soul and never can. It is a sense of contentment that I can rest now. I don't have to prove anything, correct anything, or fear anything. I am IN the care of the Lord. I surrendered myself to this process, and I don't need huge amounts of food to feel this way. I have ENOUGH!! He is ENOUGH!!

(And now Tim has enough, eternally wrapped in the arms of our Lord in heaven. I'll see you again, gentle one.)

Myth # 14

It's too late to offer help.

Lots of addictive habits affect those you love. Drinking, drugs, gambling, anger, irresponsible spending, all put sorrowful dents into a family's hopes for healthy living. However, for years I rationalized that my eating patterns only affected me.

Then I read a verse from Hebrews: *"By faith, Noah, in reverence for God, prepared an ark for the salvation of his household."* (Hebrews 11:7) The part that hit me right between the eyes was "Prepared an ark *FOR THE SALVATION OF HIS HOUSEHOLD.*"

Noah spent an entire year laboring to build an ark so that his family would be saved from the corruption of the world. As I am starting this year saying, *This is the year I will get a handle on my weight issues – this is the year* – I think about Noah. This was the year that he labored intensely surrounded by great mocking and scoffing and the temptations to quit – because it was for his family.

It's a myth that my food choices only affect me.

My entire family struggles with weight issues, so I feel immense guilt. I taught them all they know! I was the parent and wife responsible for the meal choices and what filled the shopping cart. I wasn't a good Noah to my family.

I'm ashamed to admit that I didn't do this job as healthy coach/parent very well at all. My girls are gone from the house now and are living on their own. While my living in guilt over my poor leadership in this area is fruitless, my creating new patterns and living by example doesn't have to be fruitless.

I need to focus on building my ark --getting the salvation from food addictions for myself and my family. Did you know another way to translate the word "salvation" in the Greek is HEALING? Noah was healing his family as he was saving them. Changes I make in my eating patterns also may work to heal my family.

Noah was saving his family from destruction. He dedicated himself to that cause. He brought them out safely to the new world -SAFE - because he focused – he labored – he chose – he committed IN SPITE OF everything around him that was telling him he was foolish. All of those years I was raising my kids, I hate to admit that I wasn't diligent in the health department. I was basically living in survival, and I settled for how I had been taught to eat.

I over-focused on the easy, good tasting foods instead of items that were healthy. I didn't want to have battles at the dinner table like we had when I was a kid.

I introduced lots of food into our home that were not healthy just for convenience sake as a busy mom.

(My mom insisted we have liver and onions once a week. My brother and I finally figured out a way to get the liver under the table to feed it to the dog!! That was only one of the food battles we experienced almost once a week in my home while growing up.)

That was then and this is now. I need to take this moment to ask my children and my husband to forgive me. The world caught me. The traps of the American abundance stole my heart. I joined right in. We ate too much, I fixed too much, it wasn't balanced, it was what they would like to eat. I brought into our home the people-pleasing of food. I brought in the Standard American Diet (SAD). As a result, I did not teach my children well.

However, wallowing in guilt won't change today. I am not looking back – but forward. I need to start TODAY to make better choices. Bad choices do catch up to us. The choices just overwhelm us, and we are caught up and trapped.

I need a new vision of what it means
to eat to live instead of living to eat..
What is healthy? What is an adequate portion?
What is balance?

Surely I need to invest time and energy into learning more about this – not only for my own sake but for my family. Every day food choices hit us. We need to make good choices a priority for our family's sake as well as our own.

Do you know what is inspiring me? A need to turn it around. To be a better example to my girls. To be a Noah of healing. When they think of their mother in regards to dieting and weight issues, they see a failure extraordinaire!! I want to set the pace of healthy change for them, not to suffer more defeat.

Someone once told me that when I was tempted, I should turn that into a prayer for my children that they may not be tempted in the same way. It is true that the sins of the children are passed on from their parents. (Exodus 34:7) Oh, Lord, may we turn the tide of this around in our families.

Romans talks about being in a cycle of sin and death (Romans 8). We get into a cycle in our families where sin repeats itself again and again – generation to generation. We look at our children and see the same patterns in them as we see in ourselves. (That's so painful!)

However, parents are the ones who need to take the stand to change those patterns, those cycles. I know many families who have begun taking drastic measures to not repeat the sins of their families. They have chosen as parents to move out of that rutted cycle and pattern whatever it may be.

I can do this for my family in regards to food choices. I can be a Noah. I'm so surprised at the number of moms who take their kids to fast food restaurants three even four times a week. What a great convenience, but what a horrible pattern we are setting in place for our children. I was even more sympathetic with some of my new friends from my "weight class" at church who say their greatest temptation is being lured into a drive-thru for French fries. Temptation lures us from every corner.

This is not a health food book, so I'll stop here. This idea of being Noah, of building an ark of healthy eating is a driving force for me. While it's too late for me as a mom with kids no longer at home to affect meal changes, I can let them see a healthier choosing mama. It might not be too late for you. I needed to ask *forgiveness*, but *you* could still *make a difference*.

NOTE: At this writing, my oldest daughter has lost 65 pounds. I'm so proud of her!!! It's not just the weight loss, she is learning about healthy eating and is committed to that change. She is reversing this cycle for her family, and is learning all about eating better than I taught her! I'm so thankful!! I'm learning from her!

Myth # 15

Food has an emotion attached that draws me in!

There is no doubt about it. My mom was right. I am a drama queen. I get emotional about everything. I have even discovered that I emotionalize foods. I have actually attached an emotional word or title to the foods I eat – or shouldn't eat – or crave!

I think, *That's a CHEATING FOOD ..... That's a BINGE FOOD.....that's a DIET FOOD.... that's an "I'm-mad-at-the-world" food ......that's a "TV-at-night- comfort" food .....that's a "when-I go-off-my diet" food .....that's a "love-myself-for-eating-it" food* and of course, *a "hate-myself-for -eating- it"* food.

Let me give you some examples. Peanut butter has got to be the greatest food created -- second only to ice cream. (Did you know that George Washington Carver invented 300 uses for the peanut, but peanut butter was his greatest.) The crunchier the better!!! I love it on sourdough bread with lots of jam. (Enough of that! I can't focus on it or I will want it.)

Over the years, though, I have put into my mind that if I eat any peanut butter, I am cheating!!! After all, it contains so much fat. Instead, I am trying to unlearn that emotional title for it by just putting a small amount on one piece of toast!! Occasionally it is a good OPTIONAL source of protein adding a good variety to my eating plan. I'm trying to enjoy it without *feeling* like I have been cheating after eating it – that I am bad

How about popcorn? Yes, popcorn has become my binge food. Not just a cup....but an entire big, big, bowl of it just stuffed into my mouth one handful after another. After a while, it begins to taste like stale sawdust...but I keep eating it. I have had to learn to make it OPTIONAL – and in smaller portions – not necessary while watching a good movie.

Celery has become a "diet food" emotionally. In my mind, you only eat celery when you are dieting. Instead, it can be a crunchy delight in my salad. That's why the other day I just stared at the stalk of celery, and invited it to take on a new meaning to me. A fun addition to my turkey and tomato stew, a great afternoon CRUNCH, and a good OPTION. Redefining foods and removing the emotion has become important to me on this journey.

Reese's Peanut Butter Cups are delicious, but I have attached an emotion to them...a STRONG emotion. When I am MAD at the world....they come to comfort...yes THEY...not just one but a handful. They are an *"I deserve this"* food! I can't just eat one. The emotional pull is so strong I LAND there far too often. I feel I *get something* from them – something unhealthy.

Now when I look at a Reese's Peanut Butter Cup, I am giving them a new title: OPTIONAL. I am learning now that there are other OPTIONS to handling the "mad at the world" events in my life. Taking a STOMPING walk usually helps. On the walk I can get some of the energy out....some of the frustration out.

I have to realize, though, that after the walk I may have to deal with the thing that is making me mad. I may need to talk with someone or make a change in some way. Stomping doesn't really STOMP the problem out, it just helps you see it more clearly. That clarity usually requires some action when I come home from my stomp walk.

Ice cream fits the bill for "TV at night comfort food" and also "love me, myself and I by eating it" food. How many scoops (or bowls) will depend upon how much love I feel I need and how much TV has captured me.

I have discovered that my deepest "in place" habit is needing something to snack on after dinner while watching TV. Eating in front of TV is like a bear trap. Almost impossible to get out of!

I want to share with you a victory the other night. Our schedule had gotten all bumped around, and I was off my normal pattern of eating at certain times. That always throws me for a loop. I was hungry for a meal....and not wanting to wait to fix something healthy. That's when I decided to have left-overs from something my husband loves but not something in my eating plan.

I pulled it out of the refrigerator, said YES to myself, warmed it, took it into the living room, turned on the TV and proceeded to eat it. That is when I thought of the word OPTIONAL. I had a choice, an option. I could eat it all, or just a few bites. I made a choice.....and later was so delighted with that choice.

I OPTED out of eating the entire thing. Three-fourths of it was left on the plate. YES!!! That might not seem like much of a victory to you, but to me with my habits of emptying the plate - it was a major breakthrough. It felt so good. I know that I can repeat that choice again and again to remove the patterns I have developed.

This was no longer an emotional plate of food. There was no emotion drawing me to it saying, *My day was thrown around so much, and now I am sooooo very hungry that I DESERVE this.* Oh, the things we tell ourselves!

Yes, even "DESERVE" is an emotional word.
I can have this one treat...I DESERVE it because
I've been so good all week.

What if we replaced deserve with need? The word *deserve* carries with it such strong emotions. We seem to be able to be more realistic with the idea of *NEED* instead of *deserve.* That's probably because I don't really NEED these things. They can be OPTIONAL.

Can you see when I am telling myself these things, that I am connecting my emotions with a certain food? Food needs to be defined as food – not as an emotion. I have found that making food neutral and optional has been a powerful part of changing my heart.

One of my friends even told me the other day that her counselor told her that she is afraid of food. She is afraid she will eat what she shouldn't. Her health is gravely at stake here, so I can understand her fear of certain foods. The reality is, whatever you fear actually controls you. A redefining of food is needed for her to not fear food.

Here's a suggestions. Ask yourself if food has emotional definitions for you. See places where you can redefine these.

If for years you have "rewarded yourself" -- "deserved" -- wanted to "cheat" -- had a "TV eating pattern" - put three scoops of ice cream into your bowl just "because you could" – have found "feeling defeated" foods, well, it is time to REDEFINE your foods. Try these new definitions: Optional! Satisfying! Sources of Energy! Not best for you! I can do better! Another time! Have a negative affect!

OPTIONAL!!
Life is all about options!

Myth # 16

That really can't be ME in the mirror!

When I stand in front of the mirror, I don't see what I think I am. Who is this fat woman looking back at me? How did this happen? And to me?

I have walked with the Lord for over 50 years. The word of God is my foundation. I love to study it. I love to serve the Lord. God has used me in the lives of others. The Lord and I have what I consider a rich relationship – except for the fat! (And the eating habits that cause the fat!) That's not really ME, is it?

I like the me I think I am much more than what I see in the mirror!

How can I handle so much of life with love, grace and efficiency and have this part of my life be such a peninsula of defeat? I want to be free from that land mass!! What I see in the mirror can't really be the real me! Can it?

In reflection as I sit here looking into the mirror seeing someone I thought I wasn't, I recall how God has worked so many miracles in my life, changing my heart in so many ways: changing my marriage, working in my children, providing for us in so many unexpected times and ways, refreshing my weary soul, giving me peace when the world around me seemed so stormy, and the list could go on and on.

How can this fat person I see in the mirror be me?   There seems like a disconnect. How can this state of my body be happening to me? How did I even let this happen? If I am so spiritually-minded, how did this fleshy thing happen?

Simply put – I've been working with God on the internal. I have given Him my soul but obviously not my body. He has worked amazing miracles on the inside – in my soul. My body, well, it seems to have been put on hold, and I admit, by me! It has been a "beside the point."

I find it easier to surrender my heart than my appetite. I kept thinking, my Spirit and soul are key in the Christian's life. I have to admit that I have also been full of convenient rationalizations: *I can't balance everything, you know.*

It's like my house. When spring comes, I work outside to spruce up the garden, pick up winter's fallen branches, put in new bark, prepare the soil for my garden, plant my garden, repair flower beds – and all that comes with the joy of spring.

However, when I pay this much attention to the outside, the inside of my house becomes a wreck. Dishes are left undone, the toilets...(well, that is a subject for another time), my laundry stacks up, the vacuuming is ignored – well, it's one or the other – work on the outside the house or the inside the house.

Yard work = dirty house. Clean house = neglected yard work. Sometimes things just get neglected.

As I look in the mirror, I see LOTS of neglect. How did I let this part of me go? Again, excuses: There just doesn't seem to be enough time for everything! Busy mother, working, ministry responsibilities, home care – it is easier to succumb to the SAD (Standard American Diet) of processed and fast foods when life is busy. After all, I'm doing spiritual things!

After a while, though, this neglect takes its toll on our health and our bodies. Finally, when some health issues arose, I knew the excuses needed to end. I needed to pay more attention to my health. I was so tired all of the time, I felt like I was aging 10 years in one year. When I talked to a new doctor about this, she heard me. (I love it when doctors HEAR you and don't brush you off.) She did blood work and sure enough my iron and Vitamin B levels were really low. She put me on an aggressive regimen to boost these up, and within six months I was saying, "I'm back!" My body had been neglected and was depleted, needing attention.

I tend to just go and go and go, and then go some more until there is no fuel left. If you add to that the fact that I was not eating right, then my body was being asked to do more than it can physically do.

How to get the balance between care for my soul and care for my body was a great source of frustration.

Paul told Timothy that physical exercise is important, but spiritual exercise is even more important. *"Take time to keep yourself spiritually fit. Bodily fitness has a certain value, but spiritual fitness is essential both for this present life and for the life to come."* I Timothy 5 :8 (Phillips translation.)

Wise words, but realistically, I didn't know how to make it all work with my busy life demands. My rationalizations needed to stop. Exercise and eating right had to become part of my spiritual walk. You make time for what is important.

I also know that I could never give up my precious time in the word. However, when I exercised in the morning, there never seemed to be time to have a rich devotional time. When

I put devotions first, I would love it so much I forgot about exercise. I found it so hard to balance them. Exercise always seem to lose out.

There had to be a way to partner with God to take care of the body and the soul.

During this time of letting my physical self go, I discovered, that the inside and the outside are extremely interconnected. Both need our attention. How we treat our bodies (our temples) is related to how we feel about ourselves –about the condition of our hearts.   How our souls are doing reflects how we treat our bodies. If I have any kind of inward "talk" to myself that devalues me, then my attitude towards my health suffers.

If I say: *"I'm not valuable," "I don't really count for much," "I can't do this," "I'm hopeless," "I'm too busy to take the time to eat healthy," "It doesn't matter, and I don't matter," "All of my family members are heavy, so I can't be any other way," "I deserve this pleasure since the rest of my life is a mess," "I'll take care of myself after my kids are grown and gone,"* and on and on it goes.

Negative talk inside = uncared-for body outside! When I started hearing my inside statements, really becoming aware of my self-talk and taking heed to it, I realized what I was telling myself about myself was motivating my choices in the kitchen. You see, the sad thing is that I was believing myself.

Sometimes I felt "I'm peddling as fast as I can. What more does God expect of me?"

Back to our original question: "How can this be happening to me?" It can –it did– and now I need to take some responsibility to go to the Lord for His resources and direction to DO SOMETHING ABOUT THIS BODY I SEE IN THE MIRROR. The mirror and the scales are not lying. My life is out of balance!

One time I lead a group for gals who said they wanted to really lose weight. They were all Christians. I was very surprised – no, I was actually shocked – that while all of them struggled with excessive weight, not one of them said they had asked the Lord for help. It was like they were saying, *I got myself into this....not I have to get myself out. I gained the weight now I have to lose the weight. I can't blame this on God, so I have to take responsibility for it myself.*

It reminds me of the very first baseball game at the newly built Marriners stadium in Seattle. The Mariners were winning by a big margin. Then the pitcher started to walk every batter. The opposition was scoring points by the pitcher just walking men into home base. The audience was getting rowdy and negative as the opposing team was up by two points. "Take him out!" the fans were yelling.

Finally, the coach called a time out and walked onto the field. The audience cheered. They knew he was going to say, "Head to the dugout!"

To everyone's shock, He didn't. He told the pitcher, "You got us into this mess, now you have to get us out."

The audience was dumb-founded. It was like saying, "Pick yourself up by your own boot straps – which of course is impossible." He couldn't do it, and the Marriners lost this first game in their new stadium.

This is what I felt that the ladies in this small group of friends was saying to themselves: *I got myself into this mess. I need to get myself out.* It was probably unconscious, and maybe the result of so many attempts to lose weight and nothing seeming to work.

Everyone in that group needed to embrace the truth I hear

so often from John Townsend and Henry Cloud:

> *"The sick mind that got you into this mess*
> *will never get you out of this mess."*

Yet, as each of these women spoke about their eating problems, they were saying *I need a self-rescue.* They fully believed their "sick mind" that had gotten them into this situation was going to be their "way out." It is not hard to see the futility of this unless you have somehow convinced yourself that YOU are your only way out.

On the other hand, I hadn't given up on God and wasn't trusting myself. Every day I was begging God for help. I knew I couldn't rescue myself. I was hopeless.

My prayers, however, were actually no more effective than my friends. It was like I was asking Him why He didn't just wave His Holy Spirit over me and presto, I would be thin.

> *I was desperate for His help,*
> *but I didn't know how to ask for it.*
> *How did I get to where I was?*
> *How did this happen to me?*

How? Stubbornness. It just seemed noble to give God my inside to change and for me to keep charge of my outside. I didn't want to give up my way of eating. I wanted to eat what I wanted to eat.

How did I get to be that woman in the mirror? A lack of surrender. By not having a clear picture of who I am, how I work as a total person, and then who God is and the total surrender he wanted from me.

God wants to be involved in the TOTAL me. It actually starts from the inside out, but involves the outside as well as the inside.

How did I get this way?
I made choices which God can now heal.

God works from the inside out. He also works on the inside and the outside together, one Influencing the other. I learned that you can't put one on hold while the other suffers. What you are on the outside is the fruit of what is going on inside. I needed to surrender both.

I also had a hard time accepting that I could never be able to get myself out of this mess.

Yes, you got yourself into this mess —what I see
in the mirror – but we have a God who has proved
himself a Savior. He saves us from ourselves!
Especially from the messes we get ourselves
into quite frequently.
It takes surrender.
Total surrender.

Myth # 17

I can't get beyond the regret of my past.

When my daughters went away to college and then eventually moved away to a larger city to take on their first jobs, I was flooded with an amazing rush of emotions. While I felt joy for them, there was an even more powerful sense of regret, guilt, and condemnation for myself as a mother. I realized how quickly those years passed; I had not been the mother I wanted to be in so many ways – in fact, in most ways.

In this struggle to keep my heart from drowning in regret, I asked God for wisdom. Since I couldn't have a do-over, moving past the guilt and shame seemed impossible. (Of course, those two things drove me to the refrigerator!!)

About this time, I read in James 1:5 that, *"If any woman does not know how to meet any particular problem, she only needs to ask God who gives generously to all people."* (Gender changed for our purposes. JB Phillips translation.)

I started asking God for wisdom, but felt at the same time that it was a little too late for my relationship with my girls. Remembering the various wounds I had inflicted on my girls from anger to emotional neglect pained my every waking minute.

This included my bad habits, especially as it related to food and emotional eating. I had passed this on – unintentionally, but none the less these destructive patterns had been readily picked up by my girls. Now I see how I could have done things differently, but my window of opportunity seems to be past.

It became sadly ironic to me that I really needed much more of this wisdom when my kids were younger - not as much now as an older woman. Now this new found wisdom was just pushing me farther and farther into regret. I saw all of the things I did wrong. Convinced it was too late, I wondered why God had not "generously" given me this wisdom when my kids were younger. Then I read on in the James verse. God will give us wisdom, *"without making us feel foolish or guilty."* Wait!! I feel foolish and guilty. Foolishness for being a Christian mother who was clueless most of those years!!! Guilty that I just didn't get it sooner.

As I prayed about this, God showed me that He was NOT the one making me feel this intense guilt.

The promise states that,
"He gives us wisdom
WITHOUT any guilt or regret."

That meant it was me, myself, and I who was pouring these feelings of failure upon myself. It took some time to fully comprehend this, but with surrender to the Lord, I was able to rise above the shame. I learned I couldn't move on without letting go of the guilt.

All of that said, you may be wondering why I am sharing this with you in a book on changing your heart towards food. Let me ask you: *What Christian woman who is overweight doesn't feel guilty, shameful and foolish?* I've never met one.

Personally, I needed to learn the skill of transferring one lesson learned to another part of my life. Over time, after my girls left the nest, I learned how to move on from regret and to cling to God's wisdom – I was forgiven!

Now, the challenge was to transfer that to my eating addiction.

> *God doesn't guiltify His children. He desires*
> *for them to confess, move on, and to gather*
> *more and more wisdom from Him.*

Crawling into a shell of guilt over my eating choices delights Satan because it takes me away from God's grace and my service to Him. Instead of moving on, I concluded in my unconscious faulty thinking that I needed to be punished for my years and years of dieting failure. I even said to myself one day, "I have had years of indulgence, so the only way to compensate is to completely deprive myself as a punishment." Fortunately, that isn't God's way!

> *John the Baptist told us in John 1:16 that*
> *from Jesus' fullness, "we have all received*
> *grace upon grace," which overpowers*
> *our guilt and shame. (NASB)*

The past 300 diets (I could be exaggerating, but maybe not!) that have failed are past history. (Is it that many? It surely feels like it!). No matter how many failures, *"His mercies are new every morning."* (Lamentations 3:23) In fact, that entire section of Lamentations is powerful for the failed dieter.

"Remember my affliction and my wandering. Surely my soul remembers and is bowed down within me. This I recall to my mind, therefore I have hope. The Lord's lovingkindness indeed

never ceases for His compassions never fail. They are new every morning. Great is God's faithfulness." (NASB Lamentations 3:19-23)

Notice Jeremiah (the author of Lamentations) stayed hopeful because of the Lord's mercy which is new, new, new everyday. However, failed dieters are regret-ers. The I Corinthians love chapter (13) tells us that God's love rejoices in the truth. His energy is sent forth to victory not in regretting the past but in rejoicing in what God can do.

His love "hopes all things" for us, and that hope "never ends."

I am the one who won't let myself move on because I keep my past failures alive. These failures are good for one thing and one thing only – to make us aware of our past patterns of failure and to be ready to combat them –never to use them as evidence against us.

The Lord does not condemn. Romans 8:1 tells us that all condemnation is gone if we are in Christ Jesus. If we live in regret, we are living in the rule book from over two thousand years ago!

The wisdom that God wants me to embrace is designed to help me move out of my defeating patterns. Those just force me right back into failure again and again. God wants to defeat the dangerous "gotchas" that have defeated me in the past. He does that by freely giving me His wisdom.

In God's master plan, He allows me to learn and grow and then to teach others what I have learned - maybe through failure - but I have learned!!! That's what I hope to do as a result of this book.

The lessons learned with my daughters and my role as a

mother – not my failure – needs to be my focus. The same is true for our weight loss journey. Mine is full of more failure than success, so that often tends to overpower my heart and mind. Instead, I need to not deny those failures.

Again, I Corinthians 13 tells us that *"love believes all things."* I believe the truth about my failure. I chose wrongly. I, however, I don't have to stay there. There is always hope in the Lord.

I am reminded of my friend whose son was severely wounded by a drunk driver in a car accident. He spent two years in physical therapy after they put a rod in his leg. He could not run again or possibly never even walk again. Yet, he was determined to do both. He wanted to play football, and it took a while for the truth to settle in his heart that he wouldn't have the professional football career he wanted to pursue. God had something else in mind.

When they were at the trial of the drunk driver who hit him, his mom told him to *"look at the man. Don't deny that he exists, and that he sinned against you. However, we are not going to stay there. We are going to pick up right from where you are and move on. The truth is --yes, he sinned against you and changed your life and dreams forever, but what are you going to do? Stay looking at that in self-pity, or move on to the something greater that God has for you right now?"*

This young teenager and his mom, who I have had the privilege of knowing, taught me some huge lessons about life. *"Believe all things."* Don't deny the truth. Yes, I wasn't the perfect mother. Yes, I have failed more times than I can count on my diet plans....

BUT God's love and hope never fail.

There is a tomorrow after those failing days, many bright

tomorrows full of forgiveness, mercy and new wisdom. I need to *"leave the past behind"* - the guilt, the regret, the sorrow for my failures - and move on to all *"that God has for me, my high calling in Him."* (Philippians 3:14 NASB)

I can start my "morning of new mercies" right now. When I told God I was having so much trouble handling the regrets of my past, He promised, *"He would give me wisdom."* In fact, the J.B. Phillips translation states the James passage like this: *"She can be sure that the necessary wisdom will be given to her." (Gender changed)*

Seek it like treasure! I did, I have, I am – it is my focus.

No longer living in regret.
Each failure is in the past.
Each day is NEW!

Myth # 18

It's Genetics!
I'm doomed to be
heavy.

How often I have heard these words: *I am doomed to be fat. My entire family is overweight!* I heard one lady at a Lose Weight Support Group say she knew God must want her to be overweight. As I recall, that was the only meeting she attended.

While it is not true for all of my family, many overweight people I know have repeated these words. They are easy words of resignation when you feel hopeless – when the battle just seems overwhelming.

I'm very curious, so I decided to look into the genetics of weight gain. I found that while there appears to be some genetic components that tend to cause a person to store fat more easily, other factors can reverse and defeat this propensity. One thing we know for sure is a quote I often repeat:

If you always blame, you
will always stay the same.

It's non-productive to hold on to the idea that genetics are to blame. Excuses get us nowhere. The way your family ate produced as many bad habits as the influence of your genes to gain weight. The amount of high fat and sugary foods available to us today plays an even greater factor than genetics. Getting into a program to get healthy and to lose those unwanted pounds is going to require turning around many facets of your life, not just genetics.

What you eat?
How much you eat?
If you exercise?
And how much you try to
excuse away your extra pounds.

Sometimes I hate that I am an adult and have to act like one! That means I make the choices for my life. I'm responsible! (Or should be!) I choose what goes into my mouth. I choose if I get off the couch to exercise.

The other day I had a horrible argument with myself. I didn't want to exercise. I remained stubborn for an hour or so, and then finally broke down and made the right decision to get out there and move my body. We had unexpected snow on the ground –enough to snow shoe in my neighborhood - which is not common at all. I put on the snow shoes and after the first eight steps I felt exhilarated. I asked myself, *Why did I put up such a fuss about getting out here and exercising?*

Research has shown that the location of stored fat and the propensity to store fat more readily can be genetic. Yet research also shows that we can overcome these deficits which work against our efforts. We can be transformed in our emotions and spirit as children of God, and we can be physically transformed as well. The efforts you give to the healthy eating project might have to have more punch to it, but it can be done.

The other day, I watched a movie on butterflies and was amazed to watch the process (put into high speed) of a butterfly coming out of the cocoon. It is usually a five hour process, at least. The struggle, the effort, the work required is to be commended. However, when that beautiful butterfly emerges, all of the pain is worth the gain.

I collect most of my weight in my stomach and my legs. Others carry theirs in their shoulders and stomach. I gain five pounds if I eat a piece of bread. (Okay, that is an exaggeration, maybe two pounds!) Sugar sends me into orbit. It awakens a sleeping giant in me. Just a little bit of sugar sends me crazily craving into the kitchen for more, more, more!

It has taken a while to learn this about myself after so many years in denial. That's the way my body works. It could have to do with genetics. I don't know. I just know that FOR ME, these are the things I need to avoid as I battle.

Some people can't run for exercise and can only do non-weight baring exercises like swimming and biking because of their propensity to arthritis or weak knees. (I tell my daughters to walk not run. Grandma had her knees replaced, and I might be headed the same direction. Our family just has a propensity to arthritic knees!) What's true for you?

Acknowledging that "this is true about me" is key. Then your exercise and eating practices can be adjusted. Excuses only hold us back. I found that stating the truths about me and my past eating routines is bringing into the light ideas that might have been defeating me in the past.

In our family we have the thin ones and the heavier ones. While my father was built nicely, he drove my brother crazy by eating butter and other fatty foods. My dad died of a heart attack a few years after having bi-pass surgery. My mother struggled with her weight as did her older sisters. Their mother also struggled with weight issues, but much of that was after having eight children.

My brother is thin and healthy. He is 70 and still skis in the winter and hikes in the summer. His better half makes sure he eats right fixing him all sorts of creative and healthy dishes. She had a propensity to being a bit overweight, but together they have dedicated themselves to being healthy, and she is now trim and fit.

Mindset and new habits
can overpower genetics.

Some of the diseases that are in our family genetics are also connected to our weight issues. Overcoming the weight issues often helps us battle the connection of various diseases. My grandfather died of a heat attack at 80, and my father followed the family course and died at 79. My brother is bound and determined to reverse the family patterns.

I also have another challenge. In my current reality, my husband doesn't want to commit to real healthy eating like I have tried to do. I have several friends who have lost weight with their husbands. I admit that I'm jealous. I need to work on my healthy eating within the context of my marriage. That's reality for me. No excuses!

I guess it comes down to our choices. We can choose excuses or to face the reality of what we have been handed in this life. Reality trumps denial any day! Bringing the truths into the light moves you closer to victory. No matter how hard your battle, you must face it like an adult. If that's "just the way it is with you," then accept that it is "just the way it is with you."

No blame. No comparisons! Jesus and Peter had a difficult conversation right before Jesus ascended to the Father. After Jesus told Peter that his future might hold some specific difficult and painful challenges, Peter questioned Jesus about John's future. *"What about him?"* Peter asked.

Jesus responded and said, *"If I want him to remain until I come, what is that to you? You must follow me."* (John 21:18-22) That is our challenge. We are all unique. We must take the challenge to individually follow him whatever our personal challenges.

No blame
or excuses allowed.

Myth # 19

I keep sinning, so I must not really be a child of God.

There is nothing more soothing to the soul than to know with great certainty that you are a child of God – that you have come into His family and are assured of His love and eternal life.

However, when things get out of hand in an area of your life, you can easily begin to question your position in Christ. When my marriage got rocky, I questioned how two Christians could be on such a difficult journey. Maybe we weren't really Christians.

Then God worked a miracle – not all at once, but over many years, and we found ourselves healed and happy in what had been a tumultuous marriage. Only God could do this and for His Glory. What an amazing praise to God to share our testimony.

With my eating patterns, however, I once again began to question the solidity of my faith. Realize this involved failure after failure on diets, binge eating, and rebellion when the voice inside me I knew as the Holy Spirit said to STOP and I kept going for the kitchen,

The words I John 2:15 (NASB) kept haunting my mind.

"Do not love the world or the things of the world. If anyone loves the world, the love of the Father is not in Him. For all that is in the world - the desires of the flesh and the desires of the eyes and the pride of life - is not from the Father but is from the world."

"The Father is not in Him!" I know there are various beliefs about eternal security, but I am not one who believes you can lose your salvation. However, when you have habits and patterns in your life like I had experienced in the area of gluttony, it is easy to begin to question this.

John said exactly what I was feeling. *How can I be of the Father and of the world at the same time?* Jesus told the disciples *"No woman can serve two masters."* (Gender change).

If I choose the world, I have lost the Father. I keep on sinning, so the love of the Father must not be in me. Either I never became a Christian or it didn't take or I lost it. That was my haunting conclusion.

What would it take, I began to ask, to really have the Lord in my life and know for sure I was a child of God? This is confusing because there are other areas of my life where I was sold out, 1000% God's woman. No question about it!! If God instructed me to do a hard thing like ask forgiveness or take a risk and boldly move out in faith, I was right on it. No questions asked. God said to do it, and I obeyed. However, I just didn't know how to define this eating issue in my life in terms of my faith and my position as a Christian.

I know many women feel this way. They are successful moms, wives, business women, church leaders, Bible teachers, and speakers. In these areas, they are very proficient and accomplished. Why not in the area of food? What is it about food that would lead to such a feeling of defeat that you would even question your salvation?

So, how did I handle this fear? I lived a life
compensating for this defeating area.

I began to deny there was a problem. I just didn't let it be a problem. It was just who I was. I overworked the good areas of my life and avoided thinking about the out-of-control issues.

Then, it all came crashing down and you know you can't deny the problem any longer. I had to admit my eating patterns were part of who I was in Christ. They were keeping me from moving on to greater maturity. The compensation game had to stop or I would be stuck here the rest of my life.

Deep in my heart there has always been the passion to be all that I can be for Christ. To grow all I can in my time on this earth. Here I am 67, maybe 20 or so years left on this earth (or more if God is gracious to me in that way), and I'm still stuck in this sin pattern. If I was truly His, truly a child of God, then there could be victory for this just as God gave victory to my husband and I in our marriage and other areas of my life. Those were my haunting thoughts.

I had to come to a point where I was willing to go there – to face it head on – to no longer deny that this issue was a part of my life – in fact, a big part of my life –probably six or more times a day. (In fact, at one point I counted that I thought about food over 300 times in a day — was tempted 300 times in one day to eat even when not hungry. That's how bad the problem became in my life!)

I had to say to the Lord, "Okay, this is the year!!"
Your way this time. Not the crazy diet
routine, but your way.

God, after all, created food and the need for fuel in our bodies. He must have "a way" to help us out of this cycle of sin and death in the area of food. There must be a right way to use this gift of food He provided for us. He must be able to show me the way He has FOR ME even in the midst of my neediness and rebellion. After all, I am surely a child of God. That can't be in question, because if it is all hope is lost.

John also tenderly offers us these words, *"My little children, I am writing these things to you so that you may not sin. But if anyone does sin, we have an advocate with the Father, Jesus Christ the righteous."* (I John 2:1 NASB)

When Jesus died, He expected us to have sin in our lives. He knows us, that's why He came. It is the "sin that goes on and on" that gets us to question our position in Him.

It boils down to this: I CAN'T DO IT! On my own I can't move on from this sin. He is the only one who can work this miracle in my life. My surrender to His power in my life is the only way. That way HE gets the glory. If we are ready to claim a victory for ourselves, He won't let the victory happen. It has to be in His way, in His time and for His glory.

He doesn't want to share the glory with some diet plan.

Our dependence needs to be entirely on Him. If we trust a plan, it would be like Joshua using the same plan again and again to have victories entering the promise land. God changed the plan from Jericho to Ai, to each new town they were to battle. That way, God got the glory, not the plan.

I think I've tried almost every diet plan there is, so I can tell you there is no glory in this. There is glory, however, when we surrender and allow Him to change our heart and to rely upon the power of the Holy Spirit.

Now, to be honest, I thought I gave over total surrender a million times. Maybe two million. (Okay, exaggeration!) However, those efforts ended in trusting a diet plan or will-power. As I look back, I see the pattern. *Lord, this time it's going to be different.* **Not** *what diet shall I use?* Instead, asking how much move of the Lord can I call upon and how can He change my heart.

I was moving toward the diet discipline more than to the surrender to Him. I hate to admit this -- 67 years of doing it wrong. That tells you how stubborn I am. How in love with my own satisfaction I am. I have one hold-out in my devotion to God – food. That's my area of control.

I feel like the Galatians when Paul notes: *"Having begun in the Spirit and now trying to be perfected by the flesh."* (Gal. 3:3 NASB) My flesh cannot perfect me. Only the Spirit of God can work this miracle IN ME.

I never could figure out why a diet tells me to not eat a food that God made. That seemed to be counter to the Lord's plan. Yet, time and time again, I went along with it. No fruit. No bread. (That one really got me. Jesus was the bread of life! I learned, though, the bread is now so processed it is not giving us the real intention of God's gift bread!)

Diets deprive.
Jesus satisfies.

We can, however, learn some tips from people who have walked this battlefield! Steve Arterburn, from the *Lose it for Life* program and New Life Ministries, suggests the "SNOW FREE" plan. Nothing white. No white bread (that has been processed to death!), no white sugar, no potatoes.

Gary Smalley, who never suffered from weight issues until he got older, suggests about the same thing. He found white sugar and flour to be culprits of weight gain in his life.

What is God's plan? I finally see it - The Fruit of the Spirit. The fruit of His Spirt of self-control. I always laughed that self-control was the last of the fruits on the list in Galatians 5:22. However, that last fruit never seemed to grow on my tree, or maybe it was just my resistence.

I have come to realize that God is in me working to change the very core of my being, my wiring, my heart, my mechanisms, as Dr. Henry Cloud calls it. When this takes place, you see yourself responding to food in a whole new way. It is no longer something you NEED. You enjoy it, but are not desperate for it.

Only God can take you to that place of a changed heart! That's when you see the power of God in your life and know you are His child Jesus made a way for us to be human. For us to fail and to be forgiven. Like John said, the ideal is not to sin. The reality is, we do. We all have areas of sin in our lives that need God's transforming power. When this process occurs, it brings Glory to God and none other.

I never have to doubt my salvation or my position as a child of God. I don't have to prove myself in Him. He definitely proved His love on the cross.

He proves Himself in me
by the transformations He performs
in my life that ONLY HE can do.

Myth # 20

As a woman, I just don't measure up!

As I have shared many times, when I was a little girl, my name wasn't Christie. It was C*H*R*I*S*T*I*E! *"Christie why are you into trouble again? Why don't you ever listen? Why are you doing that again when I told you not to? Why can't you just stand quietly?" "Don't you ever listen or obey?"*

(I hope you can catch the attitude behind these words. When I share this as a speaker, the audience gets a kick out of imitating me saying, "C*H*R*I*S*T*I*E!!!" with a definite attitude!)

Of course, I didn't hear those actual words in my interpretation. Instead, I heard the roaring words of judgment coming at me, "Shame on you. You are bad!" You see, to me it was never what I did that was bad. I was bad. I was wrong. I was causing problems for everyone.

The symbol that comes to mind when I remember back to these days, (which I do quite often as it became such a huge part of who I was and what I thought of myself) was a pointing finger shaking up and down, as if to say, "Naughty, naughty! Bad girl!" (Like you would do to a dog.)

When this happens often enough, I began to *FEEL* the pain of these words. Then I began to *BELIEVE* these words. Eventually, I began to *BE* what those words suggest.

For me, it translates into I AM BAD.
When the eating issues are added then,
I AM REALLY BAD.

*(So...I ask you.....why shouldn't I go into the kitchen
and sneak food to make myself feel better?
After all, I am bad, so why not live up to who I am?)*

I remember vividly when I was in middle school, so about 12, I was searching for my real identity. *Who was I really?* Up until this time, I had received my identity from my family's many "CHRISTIES" (coming from my parents, aunts, uncles, brother, cousins, even family friends). I also formed my identity from school friends, and there were many rejections and hurts there as well.

Is it any wonder that I wanted to find out what God felt about me? Was I "CHRISTIE!" to Him? Okay, I'm going to confess to you the crazy thing I did to get an answer to that question. (I was a middle-schooler, so take that into account). I went outside one evening at dusk and looked up in to the sky. I fully believed I would be able to see God. I asked, *"What do you think of me?"*

I will never forget the vivid picture that came into my mind. I saw a finger, God's finger, shaking up and down at me, just like the "shame, shame" finger that said "bad girl." It was accompanied by the shaking of the head (no, no) and the sound of "tsk, tsk."

What a shame. Where did that come from? It certainly was NOT from the God of love who created and died for me. It was certainly one of Satan's deceptions. None the less, this lie of God's opinion of me stuck with me for years. The idea others had of me had been so deeply embedded into my identity and soul, that I could not see God as He really saw me.

I projected the responses of others onto God. It haunted me every time I made a mistake or didn't do something up to someone else's standards. CHRISTIE! CHRISTIE!

Comfort has to come from somewhere when this feeling overwhelms you. When it should have come from the Lord, for me, it came from the kitchen. From sneaking sugary and forbidden foods.

Food became my place of acceptance. Food never judged me. It became a great escape from condemnation. This pattern of going to the kitchen to feel accepted would continue until, well – many pounds later. I have to admit, food was an idol to me.

Then the Lord began to do a work in me and through others to show me His love and acceptance. He replaced the old wrong image of Him with His true image.

The first replacement involved that finger motion. Remember I saw God shaking his finger at me. As I opened myself up to learn more what God is really like and how much He loves me, the "bad, bad girl" image was replaced with "I created you to be just who you are -- inquisitive, outgoing, friendly, caring, wanting to know, risk-taker, curious, creative, and an explorer."

I am all of those things and God made me like that. With those qualities, I have started two businesses from scratch. I have a degree in journalism, so I am always asking "who, what, when, where, why and how?" (It drives my husband crazy!!) I am often the first to try something and then tell my friends about it. I never stop learning and growing! All of these qualities that used to get me into trouble as a young girl, God now uses to serve Him.

In my mind, His finger no longer says, "shame on you." Instead, the finger motions for me to come to Him. He wants me just as I am. He wants me to be who He created me to be. His call is a tender calling from a Lord who loves me, appreciates me, enjoys me and celebrates me. What a delightful change of identity!

I no longer feel I need to punish or reward myself with food for who I am.

I am the special person He created me to be – with a few extra pounds to love (that are coming off gradually)!!

The second tender expression of love also came from a significant event to me. It seems like every time I shared something or did something, people would "lean back" in doubt, disgust, scepticism, or judgement. Their body posture said, "You're weird! What you're doing is stupid! What makes you think you can do that? Who do you think you are anyway? You can't do that. CHRISTIE! can't do that!! Don't even try! That's for someone – well -- smarter and better than you. Someone not as fat!"

That was until the day I was at a retreat. Something happened one evening at that retreat that I will never forget. It changed my life and my self-identity.

The leader asked us all to close our eyes and to try to picture God's holiness and glory shining down on us. (Remember, the last time I did this, I saw the "naughty, naughty" finger being shaken at me. Needless to say, I was a bit nervous to try this again although it had been years.)

I closed my eyes (which took courage at first as I was afraid of what I would see) and immediately I saw a brightly glowing area. In the middle of this area was a throne where Jesus was sitting.

The look on His face was one of pleasure, happiness, enjoyment, adoring – towards ME!! In my image, I saw myself standing right before him and His face was looking straight at me.   Then I heard Him say to my heart, "I enjoy doing life with you!" Those were golden words. (I remember one of my girlfriends who is a counselor to youth telling me that kids don't want to know if you love them, they want to know if you enjoy them.)

Jesus was enjoying ME!! I can't remember anyone ever saying they enjoyed me!

It was then that the picture in my mind changed. I watched as His body started to lean towards me. My heart stopped. Then, with a gentle smile on His face, He leaned in to ME!! This was a glorious and healing gift to me.

It was a genuine expression of care and interest – an acknowledgment that I was a person of worth. (Each time I think about this I cry.) Yes, I will never forget that experience. It changed my life and my choices.

I have experienced this amazing feeling of being "leaned into" one other time, and the sense there was also profound. I had the privilege of attending an *Ultimate Leadership Conference* with Henry Cloud and John Townsend. www.cloudtownsend.com. (I highly recommend this highly personal, life-changing, week-long experience!)

While Henry and John spoke to us as a group several times a day, we were also placed into a small group that remained our group for the entire week.

Our eight-member group met together with a therapist about

ten times over the week. Each time we met together several of us had the opportunity to share about our lives, usually areas that were painful and needed some healing.

An amazing thing happened each time I shared.
The group LEANED in toward me.

It was like love was gushing out from them towards me. Jesus loving me through them. Their love. Their caring. Their acceptance. It was beautifully overwhelming.

They leaned in to me like Jesus did in my picture image. They were being "Jesus with skin on," an expression Henry and John use quite often that has become dear to me as well.

Because of my past, I am very sensitive not only to the tone of people's voices when they speak to me, but also to people's body language. Leaning in speaks a million words of love, care, and acceptance to me.

When I was at the conference, I had breakfast with a gal from another group. She shared with me something interesting about this "leaning in" idea.

She said that her pastor had come to this conference in the past . He came home to tell his church staff about an eye-opening experience he had at the conference in his group. He shared this story:

In the proper context of the group meeting, one of the gals in his group of eight boldly told him (in love) that as a woman she would have a hard time working under him. He asked why. She shared with him, "Did you notice that when the men in the group shared, you leaned in to them. However, when the women shared you sat back?"

What body language! I knew exactly what she was saying. That body posture told a lot about his opinion of women. It spoke a million words of scrutiny.

Yes, in this society, being a woman often puts us in a place of being "lesser." We feel it. We are not "leaned into." Instead, we are scrutinized, and that makes us feel judged and not an equal although both men and women were equally created in the image of God.

We form prejudices about people all of the time. Not just because of race, religion or age, but because of gender, too. Women feel this a lot.

Men evaluate us with their eyes, their minds, their prejudices, and we sense it. Is it any wonder that it often drives us to feel "less than," especially in the church?

Many of us, when treated like this, are driven to try to prove ourselves. Others give up and head to the kitchen saying, *What's the use. Because I am a woman, I'll never be fully accepted in the way I want to be.* We feel marginalized, scrutinized, less than, unable to measure up, evaluated by an ungodly standard, put down and end up saying, "what's the use?"

Sometimes we even gain weight to get back
at the men who treat us "lesser than."
We may do this unconsciously,
but I propose it is one of the
reasons women are overweight.

As I moved to the place in my walk with the Lord where I recognized that HE was leaning into me – that He was saying with his finger and even His entire hand, "Come to me!" – that I was a person of value and worth, the world's opinion decreased and His opinion of me came to the forefront. I don't have to live my life proving myself.

Healing comes when we don't react to the finger pointing

and body language of the world,   and only listen to who God says we are –   His chosen, His creation made in His image (just as any man is), His gifted child, His beloved, adopted, child of the King.   We are of value – body, soul, mind and spirit. He leans in to love us.   In turn, we need to lean into him!!   In taking on His value of us, we believe it of ourselves. We become what we believe.

He enjoys us!!!
We are enjoyable!

Myth # 21

I will never let myself go over a certain weight.

When I was in college, I had to write lots of research term projects. Some teachers required that we put each fact we collected for our projects on separate 3 X 5 cards. That was a lot of work, and I'll never forget the day that my huge stack of 3 X 5 cards (which were all organized) fell all over the dorm room floor. I said to myself as I was crying and picking up all 362 cards, now-out-of-order all over the floor, *There has to be a better way!*

One professor even required that we take butcher paper and make a chart of every character in a novel we were reading. My chart was 40 feet long, and I had to crawl around on the floor to work on it. As I was crawling around on my knees from one part of the chart to another, I was once again asking myself, *Isn't there a better way?*

There has to be a better way.
I'm sure there's a better way.

That is when I developed what I call the "Miller Method." I teach this to my students, and they really seem to love how it works to help them "work smarter and not harder" in writing their research term project. (Yes, I assign one a year!)

Now, why I didn't ask myself this question when I was failing at diet after diet is beyond me. "Isn't there a better way." Even when I heard the statistic that 90% of dieters who lose weight gain it back and more, I didn't ask that question.

In fact, I couldn't believe that statistic, but as I watched my scale move slowly down and then creep back up again – past where I was before I went on the diet – and time and time again, I became a believer. That's when my "There has to be a better way" quest finally kicked in.

In the process over many years of slowly coming to this realization, I would look at the scales as they rose back up, and I'd say to myself, *I may be overweight, but at least I know I will never get higher on this scale than XXX lbs.* However, that "XXX" got higher and higher every time as I went soaring past my "promised to myself" weight limit.

I was out of control, and *There had to be a better way.* God was gracious to me once I was open to that better way – what I call *His* way for me. God will make a way, but He takes His time waiting for us to come to that point where we are ready. He had to let me exhaust every rule, diet, plan, promise, fancy eating method, latest fad, pill-power, miracle Dr. Oz treatment, etc..

All of these had one thing in common. They offered a program of self-denial. They asked for depravation. They focused on the outside behavior. They were based on laws. Jesus Christ came to change us inside out! That's how success overcoming our overeating patterns begins.

Paul tells us in Galatians that being told NO to something makes our human nature want it all the more. (Galatians 5:16-26) Our self-control can only hold out so long. We can maybe last two weeks, two months, or even two years (my record) – but our self-discipline will finally fizzle out.

He works from the inside out.
He wants to change our heart,
and until that happens our behavior
really won't change.

After my two year stretch on one diet plan, I finally got tired of eating the same old food. I needed variety. I couldn't understand how God created wonderful fruits, for example, that were denied to me on this diet.

(I won't call vegetables wonderful as I don't like many and never have! I have to admit, though, now that I am learning to use more natural spices and seasonings some of the vegetables I dreaded most have even become acceptable. I will never say that about spinach or brussel sprouts, but others like zucchini and cauliflower, have recently been making it to my plate without trying to feed them to the dog like I did as a child.)

Back to the promise to myself: *I will never get past XXX weight.* It started as a high school girl. I'd say to myself....." Never over 150 - then 160 - then 180 - then 200 - then 210. I knew something had to change when I hit 235 on the scales. *There had to be a better way.* That statistic about dieters gaining more after losing is true. I am living proof. (As are a lot of my other friends and fellow strugglers engaged in this diet routine.)

There is a better way. God changing my heart. Learning to live in the power of the Spirit. Realizing my triggers. Exchanging the world for the Lord in my thinking, my heart attitudes, and in the definition of who I am. Let me just review a couple of "better ways" that have been mentioned:

1. Let go of the need to lose weight fast. If I lose five pounds a month, I'm doing well. It needs to be a life-style of healthy eating. In fact, after a year, I realized that I lost 20 pounds overall – with many ups and downs. The final count after the dust cleared was a loss of 20 pounds. Praise the Lord. My heart was changed on the inside, something unseen except to me, and on the outside, I had lost 20 lbs. Now on to a new year! Slow and steady with a changing heart and habits!!

2. *Eat a variety of God's foods.* I shop the outside of the store which usually includes the non-processed foods. I eat lean meats, fruit, vegetables, eggs....anything God made without the processing. (Now, I have to admit, I have a few exceptions to that. I do read labels, though, and really try to stay away from any food where the label of ingredients tells me something I can't pronounce. Also, I stay away from items with added sugar, which is almost everything processed or canned right now. When they take out fat, they put in sugar. Even the low-fat sausage I used to buy has added sugar. Sugar added to sausage! Why??? (Because taking out the fat changes the flavor and adding sugar makes it palatable.)

3. *Eat only when you are hungry.* I have had to learn to discern what this means over time. I don't let myself get too hungry (or too full). Usually I eat a healthy breakfast, a mid-morning snack of a piece of fruit, a healthy lunch, an afternoon snack of nuts or a smoothie made from fruit and whey powder, and then a nice healthy but smaller-than-before dinner. I stop eating in the evening and watch the time. I don't eat again until 12 hours later to give my system a rest.

4. *I preplan my eating for the week*. One day a week, I fix meals for the week after shopping with a list so I am not tempted to buy what I don't really need. Walking into a kitchen without a plan spells danger for me.

5. *Plan diversions!* When I get focused on eating something that I shouldn't (and it can be an all-consuming focus), I need a diversion. I created a basket of diversions written on little cards. I have it right by the kitchen. That way, if I start to the "danger room" I can pick a card instead and be redirected.

Just saying NO doesn't work no matter how popular the "Just Say No" slogan is. I can't say NO without a diversion!! I know myself!! My habits are too ingrained even at this point. Maybe someday – but until then, my guard is up.

Part of my diversion is using this little phrase: SEE - SAY - SAY. SEE what it is that is driving me, bothering me, frustrating me. Then SAY "NO!" to being pulled into this trap.   Then SAY "YES!" to something other than eating.   I draw a diversion from my basket.

6. *Continue to work through the wounded areas of your heart.*   One of the things I did was to create a three fold poster board with sticky notes on it. This board is divided into time periods from my life: my childhood, my single years, my marriage life, my parenting years, and now my adult empty-nest life. (I don't think I will ever retire.) When God puts a particular trigger on my heart, I follow His guidance in how to receive healing. Sharing with my small group, reading a book, seeing a counselor, talking to someone who has had the same experience, etc. This involves being intentional in my growth.

These are all "better ways" and are baby steps that are do-able. Instead of making unrealistic promises to myself that only brings on condemnation, I realize that having my heart changed so that my behavior will change takes time. God is in no rush. He will let the scale (my weight) go up and up and up, beyond what I ever wanted, until I am ready to ask Him for help, for a changed heart and for lessons on how to walk in the Spirit.

Paul reminds us that *"If you walk in the Spirit, you will not fulfill the lust of the flesh."* Galatians 5:16.

If you are seeing the scale get way above what you ever expected, baby steps are needed towards a new heart – immediately!

Myth # 22

No one ever loses weight and keeps it off !

When I realized my blood pressure was a bit elevated and my doctor recommended taking blood pressure medicine, I was devastated. My family, at least on my mother's side, is known for low blood pressure. I never thought I would have a struggle with this, and my pride soared with a sense of *This can't be happening to me!*

I asked the doctor, "What can I do to get off these meds?" He said, "Well, you can lose weight." I figured that was coming. However, I was very surprised by his follow-up comment. "But no one ever does." I was shocked! Why would a doctor say that? I left his office feeling defeated!

About the same time, I went to the gastroenterologist as it was time to have my first colonoscopy (such a delight!). This doctor and I also had a conversation about my overall health. He said the same thing. "You'd be better off if you lost weight, but I have never known anyone to lose it and not regain it." Not again! This was so discouraging.

Then I injured my knee (getting out of my kayak in heavy waves - can you believe it?). I needed surgery on my meniscus. While looking at my Cat Scan, the orthopaedic surgeon remarked that he saw the beginnings of arthritis. That was also a family trait being passed down. My mom had to have two knees replaced, and I watched her go through this grueling event and all of the agony that came with it!

Since I didn't want to have to face the same fate, I asked him, "How can I prevent or delay the arthritis from getting worse?"

He replied, "You can lose weight,

but no one ever does!"

Really? A third time!

I was getting a very strong message here from three doctors. I could hear myself say, *If what they are saying is true, then why even try?   What is the use?   I'll just gain it back.   Even the doctors admit this! I might as well succumb to the inevitability of being fat forever.*

Why even try? I'll tell you why! Because what these doctors said about having no hope IS A LIE, and I believed this lie.   If you believe it, you are denying the truths and promises the Lord has declared over and over again.

Dr. Henry Cloud was the first Christian leader I ever heard say, "THERE IS A WAY OUT! He noted that God can rewrite our internal hearts.   Our mechanisms can change.   We can overcome! God will make a way." (In fact, Dr. Cloud has a great book by that title.)   When I heard these words, a new sense of hope revived my heart.

I remember hearing one diet guru say years ago that she can now eat three *M and M candies* from a package and be content. Impossible I thought. Totally absurd. I'd eat one entire package and crave another! Or I'd just by the party-sized package and devour that!   She even said that people left food on their plates when eating out at a restaurant. They were full, and didn't need to eat it all. While I was eyeing what they left so that I could eat it, those words and that concept seemed foreign to me.

Yet Dr. Cloud was declaring IT IS POSSIBLE. God promises

He will make a way!   My future can have a time when I will say *no* to seconds of ice cream, that I will not *want* to consume large amounts of chocolate, and not want to have *another* meal after just finishing one.

There will be a day. It is possible. I will someday be able to make chocolate chip cookies and not eat them all before serving them so that I have to make another batch!!!

YES! YES! YES!! How is this possible? I need this kind of transformation and FAST!!! Where do I sign up for that result?

Where?   With the Lord who lifts us out of the cycle of sin and death and renews our minds. With the Lord who transforms us --TRANS -- FORMS - which means He takes our "form" (That body we don't like) and forms it across to a new and beautiful way. These doctors left out the Lord and His heart-changing focus. The Lord boldly claims that YES, we can lose weight, and many of God's people have to bring His glory! He can rewire our thinking and our desires. He will put new desires into our hearts.

I am not speaking trivial "Christianese" here. You may have heard these promises many times. Well, hearing is one thing. Participating in the process is another.

I am just saying that I have seen this take place in me for the past year. It is a process. It is never instant. It is a struggle to end all struggles. But it CAN happen.

It does not come from starving yourself,
from striving,   nor from will-power.
He changes your heart.

Every day I see my heart changing. Everyday I ASK for Him to do this miracle in my heart. My desires, and my NEED for food diminishing. I have a new outlook, changing daily, over time.   Baby steps, but in the right direction.

In this process, there was a verse that confused me. *"Therefore, if anyone is in Christ, he/she is a new creation. The old things have passed away; behold, new things have come."* Why, though, if you believe in II Corinthians 5:17, is it taking so long?

I have struggled with this verse for years. If this verse is saying that I *am* a new creation and that old things *have* passed away, then something didn't "take" in me.

Some have tried to convince me that this verse means that I am a new creation, and these old sin problems shouldn't be bothering me anymore. That can't be true, as Paul explains in so many other places in his letters that we have to continue to "put on," to "shake off," and to "leave" those things which are destructive in our lives.

He admits that some areas of our lives will still dog us as we walk out our faith with Christ. Hebrews 12 tells us that we have a sin that "so easily besets you." The battle is ongoing.

So what does this *"new creation in Christ"* verse mean? The verse uses the expression *"old things have passed away."* After some research into the verb tenses involved in this verse, I found it to really means "are passing away."

Let me put on my English teacher hat here for a moment. The verb PASS AWAY is an imperfect verb. That means the process is ongoing. We aren't "perfect" yet = imperfect.

While the verse the way it is stated sounds like "POOF" all is new, the verse is really suggesting that a new process has begun.

SO what is new? What is NEW about being a NEW creation

in Christ?   Two things for sure. When you enter into a relationship with Christ, all things are new. One day you didn't have the living, powerful, personal, loving God in your life, and the next minute after receiving Him you do. Also, in this new relationship we can utilize the NEW resources now available to us

I believe what II Corinthians 5:17 is saying is that NOW that Christ is living in us, we have resources that others do not have to fight this battle – we have all sorts of new "resources" available to us. Heaven has come down into your life. However, I admit, so many times when I started a diet, I didn't use my "resources" in Christ.

This offers me so much to have victory in the battle between the old self and the new, heart-changing, self. First of all, everything that Christ accomplished on the cross is available to us. His forgiveness, His peace, His caring, His grace, His truth, His healing, His power, and especially His way of looking at us. We are now covered by His righteousness; now we are full of His grace. He has given us a new way of looking at our lives -- and our failures – even our failures with food.

We forget this! Instead of living in a hurting world with our wounds and fears, we live in a world where the Holy Spirit empowers us as He lives in us. He heals us. He gives us His presence, guidance, and partnership. These are the greatest resources available. I can do something to change food's power over me. I can call upon every resource available to me in Christ.

Satan would like you to believe that there is a can't-recover-from-this theme of blame, shame, and guilt in repeating a sin over and over again. My experience is that I am a binge eater. I stuff food into my mouth in a very ungodly fashion. However, that's the old me acting out and not taking advantage of the resources available to me.

To be quite honest here, in the past my frustration over this verse telling me that I was supposed to be a "new creation" has caused me to just stop confessing my sin. My first stop was to the shame station, instead of to the train station that will take me to the throne of grace. I hear that accusing, lying voice whisper to me – *What! How can you even think that He will keep on forgiving you? Obviously something didn't TAKE because you aren't NEW. Your oldness is still defeating you.*

When I believe that, Satan has won. He doesn't want me to see or to utilize the resources available to me.

Christ's sacrifice on the cross offers me forgiveness, and there is no shame in asking for forgiveness a million times – even a million times an hour! There is no shame and hopelessness in sinning the same sin again and again and feeling that the NEWNESS in Christ has worn off in this area. The resources are *not* going away. We just need to start each new day, each new minute renewing our focus on Him.

I used to think that if I sinned and then confessed, that sin wouldn't be a part of my life any more. That area would be NEW. Like a move from CONFESSION to PERFECTION. It didn't take long to realize that was the furthest idea from the truth.

We are on a journey to be like Christ, but we are so far from that goal, that every day we have to acknowledge missing the mark through confession knowing that the journey is ongoing.

The reality is, my walk does not look like a straight line from sin to confession to perfection. My walk actually looks like a road we used to travel when going to our friend's mountain cabin. Up and down and up and down and right and left and up and down. (Yes, I got sick many times!)

Confession is another resource that I have and need to utilize. It gives mercy and a fresh start. I need both of those on this journey. When I confess, I claim all of what Christ did for me. I utilize the "heavenly power" that He has put into me. I have newness I can call upon.

Remember, the II Corinthians 5:17 verse actually says, "old things ARE passing away." When we confess, these "old things" are being brought out to the surface of recognition –into the light. That is the process of "passing away" in motion.

The other day, my kitchen was invaded with tiny, pesky fruit flies. My daughter told me about an easy way to get rid of them. What a great idea, I thought! However, if I just KNOW the method and don't DO the method, the fruit flies are going to continue to feast on my fruit and be pests in my life. If I go through the process of trying her suggested method, I can be rid of those pests. She gave me a resource, and I needed to use.

My overeating is a bit more complex than those pesky fruit flies, but the principle stands true. I can believe Satan's lies , or I can start taking the baby steps of calling upon the powers that now live in my heart. They are released with confession, and I can confess, confess, and confess some more.....confessing myself right into victory. Confession opens the door to grace, power, mercy and all that I need for this difficult journey. It's gradual --it is the old passing away not just with time but with utilizing God's resources. It's the NEW creature in the process of coming forth.

In Conclusion

"Greater is HE!"

When all is said and done, battling our weight issues is a worthy cause. No matter how defeated and discouraged we are, GREATER IS HE! I just picture that when I get to heaven, Jesus will be there to greet me. "Well done," is what I want Him to say to me.

I don't want to have to say to Him, "But I failed in this one area." I want to say, "THANK YOU for the victory."

It all boils down to SURRENDER. Yes, when all is said and done, it was my stubbornness that kept me trapped. My stubbornness to hold on to my ways, my wants, my need for control in some area.

I know what to do. I know I have a limbic system that needs transforming, and I know how God delights to help me with that! He'll move the old out with His love moving in – shown through the love of others.

I know my heart and not my behavior needs to change first. I know that determination and my will cannot fight this battle. There has to be a whole lot of crying out to God!

I know I will need to choose to go through my problems and not deny or numb them with food. He will never let me travel this journey alone.

All of this takes awareness. I had been living in a numbed world, a surrealistic world for so long with my eating binges that I wasn't aware of much. My reality was limited. Becoming more aware of HIM and HIS presence – aware of the people He sends into my life – aware of me and how I feel – this means waking up to life each day with my eyes wide open to my realities.

This means talking to God and calling out for His help OUT LOUD. No more quiet attempts inside my "self" that doesn't have what it takes to defeat this enemy. Satan can't hear my thoughts. He does hear me when I say, "NO! You aren't going to mislead me this time."

In addition to all of this, quick weight loss can't be the priority.

What if this battle was the battle you
were called to fight to prepare your heart
to more closely walk with Him.
To better prepare you for heaven
and intimacy with Him for eternity.
What if?

It's not something we can brush to the side. We need to engage fully with this battle. Out of it could come amazing growth and new depths of understanding of God and His love for us.

God's blessings on this journey. I pray that my discoveries have encouraged and exhorted you to choose the next right. Today begins with a choice, and the entire day is lived out in choices.

It begins with a decision.
Is this your year?
I pray it is!

> *In writing this book, I soon realized that I had too much information for one book. As a result, this information has been put into two books. The second book is called:*
> **50 Ways Out For Godly Women Who Are Overweight**
> *Publication date is spring of 2017.*
> Remember the *Feelings Discovery Chart* can be printed from
> **www.FreshLookThinking.com**

Books and Christian Leaders Mentioned In This Book as Well as Places to Go for Help and Counseling (most for free!):

Drs. Henry Cloud and John Townsend

The Power of One, Boundaries, Changes that Heal. How To Have A Best Friend Forever, The Entitlement Cure, Hiding from Love, Integrity, and How We Grow.

Both of these authors can be reached on their web page:

www.cloudtownsend.com

In addition to their books, they offer free online answers to thousands of questions. You can enter a topic and watch a 7-10 minute answer from these two very wise Christian psychologists. They also offer the Ultimate Leadership Conference.

Dr. Larry Crabb

Christian Psychologist and author.
Inside Out and The Safest Place on Earth..

Andy Stanley

Videos on various topics. He is on the NRB Christian TV network every Sunday Morning. You can also listen to or purchase his DVD's.

www.yourmove.is

Michael Dye

The Genesis Process. **www.genesisprocess.com** I recommend that you gather one or two (or a few more) friends together and go through this 20 week study. Purchase The Genesis Process for Change Groups, Book 1 and 2, Individual Workbook. The DVD is also available. I highly recommend this for yourself but preferably to do as a small group study. Pray, and God will provide a friend for this.

Steven Arterburn

His book *Walking Into Walls* talks about stubbornness.
New Life Live radio show - you can call in and receive free counseling on the phone. **www.newlife.com**
New Life TV - is a monthly subscription for $9.95. You can access counseling programs on your computer 24/7 discussing hundreds of topics from top Christian counselors. **www.tv.newlife.com**
Lose it for Life video series (Ebay) and now the *Living Light Workshop.* **www.newlife.com**
They also offer suggestions for counselors 1-800-NEW LIFE.

Mark Gungor

Laugh Your Way To A Better Marriage book and video.
www.MarkGungor.com

For other books and devotionals by Christie Miller
please visit her web page at **www.FreshLookThinking.com**
or email her at **Christie@FreshLookThinking.com**
To hear about Christie's drama program, visit
www.CreativeYouthTheater.com
To hear more about Christie's speaking ministry and training
to become a speaker, please visit **www.NWSpeakers.com**
To learn more about Christie's English classes and mentoring
program, please visit:
www.HomeSchoolLearningCoach.com.

61892755R00107

Made in the USA
Lexington, KY
23 March 2017